O MY PEOPLE
God's call to society

Outlook Books

O MY PEOPLE
God's call to society
John Ferguson

BY ALL MEANS
New approaches to group Bible study
William Metcalf

HOW TO READ THE BIBLE
based on the Good News Bible
John Goldingay

Other titles in preparation

John Ferguson

O MY PEOPLE

God's call to society

Oliphants Outlook Books

Cover painting 'The Lamb in the Midst of the Throne' by Adam Russell. An illustration from the book *Survival* by William Freel, published by Berrico Productions Ltd.

The poem *Reflection on Wholeness* by Amba Oduyoye originally appeared in *The Nigerian Christian*, published by The Daystar Press, Ibadan.

The lines from Dorothy L. Sayers *The Zeal of Thine House*, published by Victor Gollancz, are quoted by permission of David Higham Ltd.

The poem *The Dilemma* by J. C. Squire is from *The Survival of the Fittest* and is quoted by permission of George Allen & Unwin Ltd.

FOR FRANK AND BEATRICE

Contents

	Preface	9
1	O my people: God's call to society	11
2	All things in common: Sharing	20
3	To the least of these my brethren: Caring	32
4	My Father is still working: Work	44
5	The earth is the Lord's: Conservation	55
6	Not by might: Decentralisation	69
7	No more Jew and Greek: The open society	80
8	Put up your sword: Nonviolence	96
9	Love God with all your mind: Education	108
10	Up to the hill of the Lord: The way forward	121
	For discussion and action	133
	Bibliography	137
	Index of biblical passages	139
	General index	140

Preface

Not much preface is needed: if this book does not speak for itself, it does not speak at all.

I am conscious that it is written white hot. I am conscious for this reason of carelessness and repetition. I make little apology for this. No harm in reinforcing something by saying it more than once; and better to be overmastered by a compulsive drive than to have nothing to say and to say it with great care.

I am conscious too of drawing on material I have used elsewhere, in editorials in *Reconciliation Quarterly*, in British Council of Churches discussions, in speaking publicly about education or nonviolence. Details of thought and expression may have appeared before; but in its appearance here it is a new presentation. I have learned much from others, sometimes consciously, sometimes through unconscious assimilation, and offer my thanks to colleagues in the BCC, contributors to *Reconciliation Quarterly* and others who have informed my thinking, and who may or may not recognise their own ideas served up afresh.

On one point I must offer a word of explanation. I believe passionately in the need for genuine partnership in society between males and females. But 'man' is the normal English for *homo* as well as *vir*, and I will not mangle the language to speak of 'chairpersons' and the like. And I will not use 'it' of human beings, or be driven to the clumsiness of 'he or she'. So it is the familiar 'man' and 'he' until someone invents something better.

I am grateful to my friends and secretaries, Lynne Fryer and Wendy Simpson, for undertaking the typing in a shorter space of time than I like to allow. Being made in the image of God, they are longsuffering and of great goodness. I am a firm believer in the index; fortunately, so is my wife, and through her ministrations an index has once again become a practical reality. For that and for all the thinking and living we have shared over twenty-five years together, I am deeply thankful, and proudly dedicate these pages to those who brought her into the world and nurtured her in it.

1
O my people: God's call to society

> Hear, O my people, and I will speak, O Israel, I will testify
> against you. I am God, your God.
>
> Psalm 50.7

God calls individuals. He called Abraham out of Ur of the Chaldees. He charged Moses to lead his people out of Egypt. He spoke to the boy Samuel. He appeared in a vision to Isaiah, who, humbled and purged, volunteered to go with a message of desolation for many and hope for a few. He ordained Jeremiah to be a prophet to the nations, and put his words into Jeremiah's mouth, so that when the prophet in despair at his rejection tried to turn aside from his prophetic role, the message turned to a raging fire within him and burst out through his helpless protests.

So Jesus called Simon and Andrew, James and John, away from their fishing to follow him. He called Levi away from his dirty financial business. He forgave the sins of a paralysed neurotic and a woman caught in adultery and empowered them to make a fresh start. He saved the lost Zacchaeus. From beyond the grave he summoned the persecutor Saul to his service.

From beyond the grave he has continued to call men and women across the centuries, from atheism or indifference into his service, from a conventional conformity to a true commitment, from faith to action. From Paul through Francis of Assisi and Martin Luther and Ignatius Loyola and George Fox to Martin Luther King and Mother Teresa and Danilo Dolci their names glimmer from the pages of history. There are countless more, whose names are forgotten, but whose spirits and lives have brought light in darkness. He still calls individual men and women, boys and girls all over the world, and they must each make their individual response.

The three great parables of the lost sheep, the lost coin and the lost son speak in unmistakable language of the importance of the individual to God. Nothing must denigrate the nature of that loving, testing concern. Nothing must detract from the necessity for each individual, when the time comes, to hear and answer.

But God's concern is not exhaustively with individuals. In the poet's vision, he sits upon the circle of the earth, and its inhabitants are as grasshoppers. The nations are as a drop in a bucket, and are counted as the small dust of the balance; he takes up the isles as a very little thing.

He is the Lord of the universe, the Creator of the ends of the earth. He looked upon his creation and saw that it was very good. He who (in the 103rd Psalm) forgives iniquities, heals diseases, crowns human beings with loving-kindness and tender mercies is he who (in the 104th Psalm) crowns himself with light as with a garment, stretches out the heavens like a curtain, lays the beams of his chambers in the waters, makes the clouds his chariot, and walks on the wings of the wind. The imagery is poetical; the intention is sure. He is the Lord of Nature. So God pleads through the voice of Hosea, that it was he, not the Baalim, who gave to Israel corn and wine and oil. So the psalmist declares that God makes the grass grow for the cattle, and wine to gladden man's heart, and oil to make his face shine, and bread to strengthen him. The Lord planted the cedars of Lebanon, and the young lions roar after their prey and seek their meat from God. So Jesus takes the beauty of the flowers as the indication of God's bounty, and asserts that not a single sparrow falls to the ground without God's concern and care.

He is Lord of history. He is known to his people through two great saving acts. Again and again he declares through his prophets 'I am the Lord your God, who brought you out of the land of Egypt.' Again and again the people of Christ refer to the Lord who brought again from the dead Christ Jesus, that great shepherd of the sheep. Not only so. He is Lord of all history.

> Are you not as children of the Ethiopians to me, O children of Israel? says the Lord. Have not I brought up Israel out of the land of Egypt? and the Philistines from Caphtor, and the Syrians from Kir? (Amos 9.7)

Moab and Edom stand under his judgement, not merely for what they do to Israel, but for what they do to one another.

> Thus says the Lord: For three transgressions of Moab and for four I will not turn away punishment thereof; because he burned the bones of the king of Edom into lime. (Amos 2.1)

Cyrus is his servant, Cyrus, a tough empire-builder and militarist, who acknowledged Ahura-Mazda not YHWH as his god.

Much of the Jewish and Christian scriptures has to do with the calling of a people. We know the names of only a few of the individual Hebrews whom God called out of Egypt, like Caleb and Joshua. Moses was God's servant, his instrument, in bringing about the exodus. But the exodus was an exodus of the whole Hebrew people. The covenant at Sinai was a covenant between God and his people. To Moses he speaks face to face. His people he welcomes as a whole. He is concerned with the quality of their communal life. The *Torah*, from the relatively stark majestic simplicity of the Ten Commandments through the complexities of Leviticus to the rich humanity of Deuteronomy, lays down a way of life for the people of God. On their relationship to the Lord and his *Torah* their nationhood depended, and still today, as for centuries, it has formed the point of unity for a scattered people. So the whole people stand under judgement for apostasy or social injustice, the two great sins which provoke the prophets' denunciation, or for a foreign policy which makes the people of God dependent on great powers.

The pride of Israel testified to his face: and they do not return to the Lord their God, nor seek him for all this. Ephraim also is like a silly dove without heart: they call to Egypt, they go to Assyria. (Hosea 7.10–11)

Similarly in his own day Jesus offered the Jewish people a way which was not the way of the guerrillas (the later Zealots), nor that of the Quislings, nor the escapism of the Essenes, but a way of nonviolent, suffering involvement. He entered the capital riding lowly on an ass to fulfil the prophecy of Zechariah.

Rejoice greatly, O daughter of Zion; shout, O daughter of Jerusalem: behold your king comes to you. He is just and bears salvation, lowly, and riding upon an ass, upon a colt. And I will cut off the chariot from Ephraim, and the horse from Jerusalem, and the battle-bow shall be cut off; and he shall speak peace to the heathen; and his dominion shall be from sea to sea, and from the river to the ends of the earth. (Zechariah 9.9–10)

His way brings peace, but as he approaches he can foresee that his people will reject his way and turn to armed uprising (as they did), and he foresees the terrible consequences, which we today see depicted on the Arch of Titus in the Forum at Rome, and weeps. For the people stand under judgement for their reliance on violence, as they stood under judgement eight centuries earlier for their reliance on great-power politics.

The New Testament – the New Covenant, as it might be more properly called – has to do with the creation of a new community, a new Israel. The old covenant had Law, the *Torah*, as its binding force; the new covenant (foreshadowed by Jeremiah) lays on the new community Love, *agape*. It is nonsense to say with some theologians that love is inoperative in a communal context; one would rather aver that, as with the *Torah*, its primary point of reference is communal. The old covenant was sealed with the blood of oxen (as the liberation had been marked by the blood of the passover lamb); the new covenant was sealed with the blood of Jesus. The old covenant was not with Moses, but with the children of Israel; Moses was merely the instrument. The new covenant is with the new Israel, the Church. The individual does not exist of or to himself; he is a limb of the body, of which Christ is the head. It is at least arguable that when Paul uses the phrase about being 'in Christ' he means 'incorporate in the Church'. If you cannot divide the Church into groups or sects, seeing that Christ is not divided, still less can you divide it into individuals. The individual finds his true self only as part of a community.

There is a powerful example of this corporate way of thinking in Christ's parable of judgement, the parable of the sheep and the goats. In this parable judgement is dependent on whether the judged have or have not given food to the hungry, and drink to the thirsty, welcomed the stranger, clothed the naked, visited the ill, and cared for those in jail. For concern, practical love for the neighbour, is concern for the Christ, and neglect of the neighbour is neglect of the Christ. The parable is often used to incite to works of personal charity, as in Frank Mason North's moving hymn 'Where cross the crowded ways of life'. But in fact it is not individuals who stand at the bar to be judged for their individual actions; it is 'the nations' who stand at the bar to be judged for their corporate actions. 'The nations' is of course often used to denote the Gentiles, but it is impossible to believe that Jesus does not intend the same judgement to apply to the Jewish people. This is not a parable about individual charity but of social justice.

The corporate and the individual are not to be dissociated in Jewish thought; they are intertwined and interdependent. The Mosaic law is at one and the same time a standard for individuals (so that Jesus can say to a young man who is asking him how to obtain eternal life 'You know the commandments which God gave Moses') and a way of life for a nation. In exactly the same way it is utterly unhistorical to treat the ethics of the Sermon on the Mount as relevant to individual behaviour but not to corporate behaviour. Such a distinction could not have occurred to Jesus's listeners; it would have been strictly meaningless to them, non-sense. Nations, communities, groups of people may be personified as a single figure. It is sometimes difficult to tell whether these mythical figures stand for individuals or groups. A notorious instance is the Servant of YHWH in Deutero-Isaiah. Sometimes he seems to be an actual historical person, perhaps the exiled king Jehoiachin, though there have been other identifications; we seem to have a portrait of an individual. Sometimes he seems a symbol. Sometimes he seems to be Israel. Sometimes he seems separate from Israel ('for the transgression of my people was he stricken'). A similar ambiguity attaches to Jesus's use of the expression 'Son of Man'. In one sense this may mean little more than a human being. But it had already acquired eschatological associations from its appearance in Daniel and in the Old Testament Apocrypha. There 'Son of Man' is certainly a representative figure, and at times seems a corporate figure. On the lips of Jesus it is usually taken to represent Jesus himself, and this is not wrong. But it has been powerfully argued that it is a corporate figure, representing the new humanity formed of Jesus and those who put on new life in and through him. The use of the singular image in this connection can be well seen in some words of Paul: 'till we all come in the unity of the faith, and of the knowledge of the Son of God, into a full-grown man, into the measure of the stature of the fullness of Christ.' At the last the crowds fall away, the disciples flee, and Jesus is left as the only representative of the corporate Son of Man, as the true Son of Man, whose stature is the standard of mature manhood.

The excessive one-sided stress on individualism from which we suffer in the Western world has been the product of bourgeois capitalism and of the Protestantism which both guided and interpreted it. It is characteristic of a limited slice of human society across a limited span of time only. It is not indigenous in mankind. For most of history and in most of the world man has had his existence only within the society into which he is born. In African tribal society a nonconformist, unless he is fey, is virtually unthinkable; he could not survive; the Nigerian poet Gabriel Okara wrote a powerful novel *The Voice* on just this theme. Individualism is in the strict sense a heresy; it exalts a partial truth into the whole truth. For there is an important truth behind the philosophies of individualism, the truth that individuals matter, that our obedience, our commitment, our love, our actions, our life matter. Biblically, this is properly seen against the background of a corporate calling. God calls Israel; in a disobedient age those who respond are the true Israel, the Remnant; in a disobedient age too God may call an individual to speak his word to his people. We sometimes think of the story of the Jewish people in the first millennium BC as the story of the prophets. This is not wrong. From them we hear the word of the Lord. They hold the key to the history. But we know of a dozen or so such prophets across the centuries. They were God's spokesmen. But we are not to suppose that he was concerned only with them. On the contrary it was because he was concerned with Israel and Judah that he spoke to and through them.

There is a further point. In the twentieth century some problems of moment can be solved only by corporate action. In the fifteenth and sixteenth centuries the world suddenly shrank. Lands unknown to Europe were discovered by sailors from Portugal and England and other nations; the globe was circumnavigated. John Donne is still excited by the discoveries.

Let sea-discoverers to new worlds have gone,
Let Maps to other worlds on worlds have shown,
Let us possesse one world, each hath one, and is one.

And again, to 'the sunne rising':

If her eyes have not blinded thine,
Looke, and to morrow late, tell mee
Whether both the' India's of spice and Myne
Be where thou leftst them, or lie here with mee.

But this is nothing to the shrinking of the world in our own century, with air travel and jet-propulsion, not to mention the development of radio and television. When I first went to Nigeria in 1956 it took sixteen hours; within ten years two thirds of that time had been lopped off. When I was appointed to the Open University I flew from America and back within twenty-four hours, and that included arriving in Glasgow instead of London in the first place, because of fog, long delays in reaching London, the formal interview and conversations with the Vice-Chancellor. We have to think on a world scale. Disease knows no frontiers; nor does terrorism. The pressures of population cannot be confined within arbitrary political boundaries. Communication has to be a subject of world agreement. The vast challenge of feeding the hungry calls for global action. And this is the work of the Spirit. For God wills that disease be healed, that the peoples know one another, that the hungry be fed and the homeless sheltered. The specialised agencies of the UN are agencies of God.

For we cannot limit the Lordship of God. To say that he is Lord of our personal lives but not of our corporate lives, Lord of the individual heart but not of politics and economics, is to say that he is not God. His Lordship is illimitable. And if God is truly love, this means that we acknowledge the Lordship of love in our politics and our economics. Reinhold Niebuhr's 'moral man and immoral society' is altogether too simplistic a dichotomy. It is also quite untrue to the Bible. It is our task as Christians to seek, proclaim and live the way of God for society as well as for individual men and women.

In October 1975 the Archbishops of Canterbury and York wrote a pastoral letter to be read in all Anglican churches. In it they asked two questions – What sort of society do we want? and What sort of people will make that society? These are important and necessary questions. But they become merely sentimental unless we couple with them a further question – What are the structures which will make possible the emergence of the sort of society we want and which will help to produce the sort of people who will make that society? It is the distinctive Christian contribution to society to seek what J. H. Oldham used to call the 'middle axioms' between the gospel and a detailed political programme. We have a deal of moral and religious exhortation, far too much government, and not enough communal energy. It is the aim of what follows to seek some of these 'middle axioms', and to explore some of the channels which might attract and focus our communal energies.

2

All things in common: Sharing

> And when they had prayed, the place in which they were gathered together was shaken; and they were all filled with the Holy Spirit, and spoke the word of God with boldness. And the company of them that believed were of one heart and of one soul; and no one said that any of the things which he possessed was his own, but they had everything in common.
>
> Acts 4.31–2

The Jews had an institution called the Year of Jubilee; there is an account of it in the twenty-fifth chapter of Leviticus. As each seventh day was to be a sabbath of rest for the workers, so each seventh year was to be a sabbath of rest for the land, when the fields might lie fallow, and the vines luxuriate. The period of seven times seven years took on a special significance. On the tenth day of the seventh month, on the Day of Atonement the trumpet was to sound heralding the Year of Jubilee in the fiftieth year. In this year all property was to revert to its original owner, who might have been compelled by poverty to sell it; so that the freehold of farmland could not be permanently alienated. At the same time Hebrew slaves with their families were to be emancipated freely. The Year of Jubilee was in this way a rebirth of the nation. It remedied inequalities; it checked the economic tendency of the rich to get richer and the poor to get poorer. It prevented the swallowing up of small holdings by large estates, in the way that proved disastrous in Roman history. The result, when it was not observed, is clear in the prophets.

> Woe to those who join house to house,
>   who add field to field,

> until there is no more room,
> and you are made to dwell alone
> in the midst of the land.
>
> (Isaiah 5.8 RSV. cf. Micah 2.2)

But the right of restoration is continually reasserted. The idea of a year of liberty (Ezek. 46.17) is a profound assertion of two beliefs: one that the land is YHWH's and the growth of unlimited estates and uncontrolled territorial acquisitiveness are contrary to his will; the other that Hebrews are brothers and should treat one another as brothers. It is YHWH's will that his people share his gifts.

Early in his ministry Jesus entered the synagogue at Nazareth, where he was brought up. They passed him the book of the prophet Isaiah, and he read from it:

> The Spirit of the Lord is upon me, because he has anointed me to preach the gospel to the poor, he has sent me to heal the broken-hearted, to preach deliverance to the captives, and recovering of sight to the blind, to set at liberty those who are bruised, to proclaim the Acceptable Year of the Lord. (Luke 4. 18–9. cf. Isaiah 61.1–2)

It is important that Jesus shut the book at this point. The next words would have been 'and the day of vengeance of our God'; this was not part of his message. The whole synagogue was hanging on his words. We have only his opening sentence, 'This day is this scripture fulfilled in your ears,' but it is enough. Jesus's coming heralds the Acceptable Year of the Lord, the Year of Jubilee, the redistribution of resources and the time of fair shares for all. It is for his people the Day of Atonement. The message is exactly that which he put in other words: 'The time is fulfilled, and the Kingdom of God is at hand: repent and believe the good news' (Mark 1.15). But the nature of the kingdom is more fully spelt out – good news for the poor, healing for those heavy in spirit, liberation for captives, recovery of sight for the blind, freedom for the oppressed, and economic justice for all.

Jesus does not provide any kind of economic blueprint; he is not that sort of teacher. But we can glean from his teaching certain attitudes which affect our economic thinking.

In the first place, in line with the Old Testament prophets, he warns against the deceitfulness of riches, the false glamour of wealth (Matt. 13.22). 'How hard it will be for the wealthy to enter the Kingdom of God!' (Mark 10.23). Treasure-stores grow rusty and moth-eaten: you can't take them with you. You cannot serve God and Money (Matt. 6.19–24). It is 'Woe to the rich!' (Luke. 6.24).

Secondly, he enjoins generosity towards those in need. The rich stranger is told to sell all he has, not as an act of asceticism, but so as to give to the poor (Mark 10.21). Zacchaeus gives half of his goods to those in need, and Jesus declares that salvation has come to his house (Luke 19.8–9). In the parable of Dives and Lazarus, part of the indictment is that the beggar was lying uncared for at the rich man's gate. He yearned to satisfy his hunger with the scraps from the table; the language implies that he did not receive even those (Luke 16.19–21). Jesus tells his host to find his happiness in sharing his meals with the poor and the crippled (Luke 14.13).

Thirdly, he insists that the riches of God's world are there for all impartially. The sun shines and the rain falls on just and unjust alike (Matt. 5.45). The Kingdom of God is like this. A man scatters seed on the ground. That is all he does. The earth produces a crop by itself; he does not do it (Mark 4.26–9). The parable of the labourers in the vineyard is here relevant. It is another parable of the Kingdom of Heaven. The landowner agrees on the usual day's wage with those who start early in the morning, and pays the same sum to those who have worked for no more than an hour. This is to be seen not as injustice to the former but as generosity to the latter (Matt. 20.1–16). Plainly the parable is making a theological not an economic point, primarily. But it would not be easy to justify large economic differentials before the man who spoke those words. The grace of God is given freely (Matt. 10.8).

The father's treatment of the prodigal is not earned by the son.

Jesus thus warns against the dangers of excessive wealth, commends sharing, and seems to suggest that God's way is egalitarian.

In the early days of the young church, after Peter and John had been arrested by the Sanhedrin and released with a caution, they returned to the fellowship and entered together into an act of thanksgiving for their deliverance, praying for strength to maintain fearlessly their witness of preaching and healing. This led to a renewed experience of the Holy Spirit. The record goes on:

> The whole body of believers was united in heart and soul. Not a man of them claimed any of his possessions as his own, but everything was held in common, while the apostles bore witness with great power to the resurrection of the Lord Jesus. (Acts 4.32–3 NEB)

This was a natural expression of *koinonia*, community, fellowship, partnership, active co-operation. This is a key-term in the New Testament. It is used in secular Greek of the same period to refer to partnership in marriage and to commercial association; there is a beautiful use of the corresponding verb in an inscription put up by a doctor to the wife who had shared both in his home and his medical work: 'You have been the only partner of my life.' John in his first letter writes: 'What we have seen and heard we declare to you, so that you and we together may share in a common fellowship, which we share with the Father and his Son Jesus Christ' (1.3). The aim of Christians is a common fellowship, grounded in a fellowship shared with Jesus and with the God whom we have seen in and through Jesus, a fellowship of active living and a fellowship which embraces others, as they take their stand upon the same ground.

Paul makes the same assertion. To the church at Corinth whose fellowship was so sadly broken he says: 'It is God himself who called you to fellowship with his Son Jesus Christ our Lord'

(1 Cor. 1.9). For Paul this was central; he expresses it not merely through the word *koinonia*, but through a multitude of verbs compounding the idea of togetherness.

> By baptism we were *buried with* him, so that as Christ was raised from the dead we too might walk in newness of life. If we are of *one nature with* him in a death like his, we shall also be *one with* him in a resurrection like his. We know that the man we once were has been *crucified with* Christ. But if we have died *with* Christ, we have faith that we shall also *come to life with* him. (Romans 6.4–8 abbr.)

> When we cry 'Abba! Father!' the Spirit himself *joins with* our spirit in testifying that we are God's children; and if children, then heirs. We are God's heirs, and Christ's *fellow-heirs*, if we *share his sufferings* now in order to *share his splendour* hereafter. (Romans 8.15–17)

So Paul makes his astonishing assertion to the Christians at Colossae that he is helping to complete what is incomplete in Christ's afflictions (1.24).

This is high theology, and rightly, for Christian action has its springs in God, and true theology finds its expression in life. For Paul is intensely practical. To Philemon he writes of a runaway slave: 'If you have me as a partner in the faith welcome him as you would welcome me' (17). The partnership is worked out in this world. So Titus is Paul's partner, not or not only in a mystical sense, but because he is sharing in the practical task of reconciling the Corinthians (2 Cor. 8.23). When Paul describes the Philippians as sharing the burden of his troubles, he goes straight on to show that he is talking of practical help, financial and other, that they have given to one another (4.14–15). He tells the Christians in Rome to express their fellowship by practical contributions to those in need (12.13). One recalls that Quaker who told an acquaintance of a sudden death leaving a destitute widow. 'I'm very sorry to hear that,' said the other. 'Yea, friend,' replied the Quaker, 'I am sorry five pounds. How sorry art thou?'

There is an admirable example of Paul's combination of down-to-earth practicality with high principle in one of his letters to Corinth. He is inviting them to extend their giving to the churches in Macedonia. He reminds them of the generosity of Jesus, who, being rich, for their sake became poor, so that through his poverty they might become rich.

Here is my considered opinion on the matter. What I ask you to do is in your own interests. You made a good beginning last year both in the work you did and in your willingness to undertake it. Now I want you to go on and finish it: be as eager to complete the scheme as you were to adopt it, and give according to your means. Provided there is an eager desire to give, God accepts what a man has; he does not ask for what he has not. There is no question of relieving others at the cost of hardship to yourselves; it is a question of equality. At the moment your surplus meets their need, but one day your need may be met from their surplus. The aim is equality; as Scripture has it, 'The man who got much had no more than enough, and the man who got little did not go short.' (2 Corinthians 8.10–15)

In that confident mutuality is the true spirit of sharing. How does Shakespeare put it in *King Lear?* —

So distribution shall undo excess,
And each man have enough.

The relationship between theology and practice was excellently put by Charles Raven in one of his books.

The Gospel is a message of fellowship. The method of Jesus was to select and train a group: the response to it was the community of the Pentecostal Church. There is no need to stress the plain fact that there is, strictly speaking, no such thing as individual salvation, *agape* implies *koinonia*, and that the Church is essential to Christianity.

The Gospel and the Church

('Church' of course means the fellowship of believers, not any particular form of ecclesiastical organisation). John Oman, the Presbyterian theologian, wrote similarly:

> What Jesus actually left behind him was a society in which no one counted anything that he possessed his own, and which occupied itself with prayer, fellowship in the breaking of bread, and evangelising. This was the first uncontaminated attempt to realise the spirit of One who had a common purse with his disciples, to whom privilege was only a call to humility in service, who found the religious sphere in the common life among common men, and who made love to God and man the sole law of his Kingdom.

Fellowship in short means community; it means down-to-earth, practical sharing; it means the literal sense of that much abused term *common-wealth*.

The secret of this is love, Christian love or *agape*. If Jesus found a faith in a Roman centurion which he had not encountered in Israel, we need not be surprised (though we should be humbled) to find elsewhere a love which we have not encountered in Christendom. But the experience should drive us back to our roots. This love to which the New Testament calls us is the very name and nature of God. God is love (1 John 4.8), and true love is seen not in our love for God but in his love for us (1 John 4.10). Yet we are called to love God, and indeed it is the natural response as we receive his love to be kindled with a love for the giver. He calls us to show the genuine quality of our response in love towards our brothers. If we do not love the brother who is set visibly before us, we cannot love the God whom we have not seen (1 John 4.20), and our professions of love are sham and eyewash. Love then will be demonstrated within the Church. When Jesus in the upper room at a moment of deep solemnity tells the inner circle of his followers to love one another (John 15.12), it is just this that he means. Love is the inner power of the new community, at once its cement and its dynamic. It is simple historical fact that the pagans looked at the fellowship of the

Church and said, marvelling at what they saw: 'How these Christians love one another!' But a love which was shown merely within a closed circle would soon turn to poison, as the Dead Sea receives rivers laden with chemical riches, but releases none, so that the riches turn to poison, the fish cannot live, and it becomes a dead sea. Such a body would not be a church, but a club, a back-slapping mutual admiration society, not a true *koinonia*. So the Christian is called to show love to the neighbour, the person of casual, accidental encounter, and to the enemy. In other words, the love which finds its expression in *koinonia* is not satisfied until the *koinonia* is extended to those outside. The Good Shepherd does not rest as long as there is one lost sheep outside the fellowship of the fold. We might extend the parable and say that he is ever seeking, like Francis, to tame the fierce wolf of Gubbio so that he may lie down with the kid.

It is shameful to have to record that the closest I have felt to this Christian way of life has been in a Jewish *kibbutz*. Here were people forged together, not by a common faith but at least by a common purpose, and held together beyond the years of pioneering enterprise and economic emergency by their experience of the shared life. Like the early Christians, they did not claim possessions as their own, though their dwellings had each its individual décor and the stamp of those within it, for true community encourages diversity. They held common resources, and common meals. The children were brought up in thier own age-groups (the exact practice varies with the different *kibbutzim*), but the hours of 5 to 7 and the whole of the Sabbath were sacrosanct to family life, and there was more genuine family closeness than in most conventional homes. All, men and women alike, worked for the community according to their gifts; tedious or unpleasant chores were shared by all so that only a small burden fell on each. The *kibbutz* traded its products outside, and the income sustained the communal life and enabled those who wished to go out into the artificial world to visit relatives, or to spend some time by the sea, or to consult a library, or to explore the capital, to do so. One illuminating fact of the familial power of true fellowship was that the young men and women tended not to marry within their own *kibbutz*, where they lived as brothers and sisters, but to seek partners from other *kibbutzniks* elsewhere, who would have similar approaches and values.

But what do we as Christians say to a society which is partially Christian?

First, we must be humble, very humble, since we are patently failing to demonstrate a better way. If we say to society at large, 'Repent' – meaning 'Change your ideas' 'Face a different way' – 'for the Kingdom of God is at hand,' we are saying the same words to ourselves.

Second, it is not for us to play down the truth we have received. God help us if we do! Whether it is received or rejected, we must go on. Like Jeremiah, we may find our message rejected. But, like Jonah, we may find it accepted – and we should not be surprised or indignant if we do.

For third, though the good news we receive in Christ is often uncommon sense, it is also often common sense. For this world, though fallen, is still God's world, and in the end can operate only in his way. We have seen the disasters brought by economic selfishness, and can point at them with cold worldly wisdom as well as hot prophetic fire. We have seen the new power coming from a society based on economic justice in China, for all its authoritarianism. Those who lived through the last world war know that there was something in the sense of common purpose then, something positive which we have since lacked. How much finer if we could recapture it in facing the enemies of hunger and poverty and disease and homelessness and illiteracy.

And fourth, our Christian insight, the prophetic word which we receive from God, does not of itself give us the technical expertise to offer detailed solutions. We can plot a direction, but unless we are also engineers we do well to listen to the experts on laying down the road surface, circumventing obstacles, tunnelling through them, climbing over them, or removing them. But equally, we must not allow the so-called experts to divert us into a different direction altogether. The terrain may be flat to the south and mountainous to the north, but if our destination is the north we must face the mountains. We do well to remember that the broad highway is liable to lead to destruction, and that the road to life is narrow and difficult.

Nonetheless, we can say some things quite clearly. We can say that the pursuit of wealth for our own prosperity is not according to the way of Christ, that the capitalist system and the gospel cannot mate together. We must protest against any way of life which puts money first. Chesterton once said that this is common to both employers and workers. No doubt, but the workers are a long way behind the employers, and learn it from them. In an inflationary age we cannot and should not expect the workers to moderate their claims for pay-increases when senior government officials suddenly receive an increase greater than the total wages of most of them. The Christian truth is short and clear. It is impossible to serve God and Mammon.

We seek instead a co-operative society. Socialism has lost some of its glamour; the nationalisation of one or two further industries is no panacea. But socialism is not the only method of developing the co-operative society; when it takes the form of state capitalism it is only remotely related to the essential changes needed.

But we have seen some movements towards co-operation in industry, notably in the Scott Bader Commonwealth. It is something of a puzzle and a shame that more Christians with responsibility in industry have not experimented with developments along these lines. The Scott Bader Commonwealth was formed in 1951 on the principles of common ownership and social equality. E. F. Schumacher said of this enterprise: 'The transfer of ownership from a person or a family to a collectivity, changes the character of ownership in so fundamental a way that it would be better to think of such a transfer as effecting the extinction of private ownership rather than as the establishment of an ownership-collective. Ownership has been replaced by specific rights

29

and responsibilities in the administration of assets.' Ownership is not based on shareholding. Membership of the Commonwealth is open to all the staff, at all levels, once they have served for eighteen months and reached the age of eighteen. No member of the Commonwealth benefits financially from his ownership. He has not contributed financially; he cannot profit from selling shares; he can take away with him nothing except his pension rights; he cannot will his ownership to another. There are no shares to sell; there is no danger from take-over bids. If the company were wound up the assets would pass to a charitable trust. By the constitution 60 per cent of profit must be ploughed back into the business (in fact the members of the Commonwealth have regularly voted for a higher proportion, to the benefit of the work rather than their own pockets); the rest is equally divided between charitable purposes and staff bonuses equally shared. Schumacher has said: 'Ownership in the traditional form has been extinguished to clear the road for a new way in industry.' This new way was explicitly an attempt to realise the spirit of Christ within a business concern.

We can further say that within society as a whole the differential of income between the lowest and highest paid members of society should never exceed a certain ratio. It cannot be a Christian society, it cannot be a healthy society by any standards, when the gap between rich and poor widens too far. Alex Wood used to say that we have not begun to realise the divisive effect of different standards of living. Within the Scott Bader Commonwealth the constitution limits the range of payment to 1:7, but in fact it is more like 1:5. Looked at coldly this still seems a wide differential. If £2,000 a year is an adequate standard of living, who needs £14,000? If £14,000 a year is a secure and comfortable standard of living, how can anyone survive on £2,000? Recognising that the Scott Bader staff are dedicated people, caught up in a common enterprise we should perhaps realistically widen the gap slightly, but surely not to more than 1:10 or 1:12. The Trades Unions have called for an upper limit of £20,000 a year; Dr. Schumacher proposes £12,000. The fixing of some ceiling would do more than almost any other measure to help us to see that we are members of the same society, and to control the fear of limitless poverty in one direction and limitless riches in the other. It would be a first step to a sharing community.

3

To the least of these my brethren: Caring

> And the King will answer them, 'Truly, I say to you, as you did it to one of the least of these my brethren, you did it to me.'
>
> Matthew 25.40

In the eleventh chapter of Acts we read that it was in Antioch that the disciples were first called Christians, first stamped with the name of Christ, first, in some sense, christened. The next paragraph goes on to tell of the Antioch Christians taking a collection for the relief of their fellow-Christians in Judaea in an expected famine. The bearing of the name of Christ goes with caring for those in need.

This was part of the evangelical power of the early Christians. They cared. They cared for widows and orphans; they cared for the sick; they cared for the hungry; they cared for prisoners and captives. Those outside said with awe in their voices, 'How these Christians love one another!', and sometimes came to join in the work of caring and in the community which cared in this way.

As the Christian church spread through the modern world in the mighty surge of missionary endeavour they took with them the spirit of caring. Wherever the Christians went hospitals and schools appeared; body and mind were cared for. More, the Christians cared in the name of Christ for those whom others rejected, for out-castes in India, for twins in Nigeria. Out of this same evangelical commitment came other changes. The most notable was the abolition of the slave trade. It is to the shame and scandal of the Christians that it took so long to bring about, and it was only when with the evangelical revival personal faith deepened that the change came. But Roger Anstey has now refuted the persuasive but inadequate thesis of Eric Williams (echoed uncritically by countless historians who have not looked at the evidence) that the abolition was due to economic changes, and has shown that it was directly linked to the abolitionists' commitment to Christ. So too at the same period Elizabeth Fry and others did notable work to humanise the treatment of prisoners. Later in the nineteenth century the Salvation Army went out to those for whom no one else was caring.

We do not seem to care with the quality of love shown in the early Church or in the evangelical revival. In 1973 a woman in Liverpool choked to death because she had nothing to eat but cardboard, and her body was not found for three months. Who cared? 300,000 pensioners need rehousing; 30,000 pensioners have no hot water and no inside lavatory. The average family spends more on drink and smoke than the average pensioners, husband and wife together, spend on food. 60,000 more old people die in winter than in summer because they are cold and hungry. Who cares? Is it any wonder that the West Indians and Africans who settle among us say that we are cruel to our old folk?

Mother Teresa, visiting London, had this to say: 'You have a Welfare State. But I have walked your streets at night and gone into your homes and found people dying unloved. Here you have a different kind of poverty. A poverty of spirit, of loneliness and being unwanted. And that is the worst disease in the world today; not tuberculosis or leprosy.'

And it is not only the old who are uncared for. The impact of large-scale teenage unemployment is to make adolescents at the most sensitive and susceptible point of their lives feel that they are unwanted by society. This is far more grievous than any economic hardship they may face by reason of being on the dole.

When Des Wilson wrote *I Know it was the Place's Fault* in 1970 he exposed a vast abyss of need. In 1966 there were 12,411 in hostels for the homeless, and 150,000 families on local authority waiting-lists in London. By 1969 the figures were 18,849 (a rise of more than 50 per cent) and 190,000 (a rise of more than 25 per cent). Today the figures are more grievous still. By the end of 1974 those in hostels numbered over 30,000, those on the waiting-lists totalled 210,000. Over eight years the number of children in care because their families were homeless had risen from 4,000 to more than 7,000. Adam Fergusson wrote in *The Times*:

That it is possible in Britain today to be literally homeless, and that thousands of families are as destitute and blameless as though an earthquake had hit them is the plain truth ... many thousands of displaced families are playing a ghastly game of musical chairs looking not only for new houses but for hovels which cannot be dignified with the name of home ... There is large scale human agony among the casualties of the system, with whom the statutory bodies are not equipped to cope.

In the mid-1960s a White Paper declared that 3,000,000 families were living in slums, near-slums or grossly overcrowded conditions. In 1967 a housing survey estimated that 1,800,000 houses, occupied by $5\frac{1}{2}$ million people, were unfit for human habitation, and 4,500,000 more houses, occupied by 13–14 million people, were below standard: this adds up to nearly half the houses of England and Wales.

Some of the Shelter reports were agonising. In Dartmouth Road they found a hostel where 22 people of mixed sexes were living and sleeping in the same room; a year later in the same hostel four families were living and sleeping together in a space about 15 feet square. At Newcastle a fifty-six-year-old sufferer from tuberculosis was living in a single room up three flights of stairs; his only lavatory was in the yard, shared with eight other people. A typical letter came from a family living in a house so damp that the clothes went mouldy and the furniture mildewed. The paintwork was peeling and the walls blackening. Open fires were unsafe. The place was infested with rats, the children ill. 'They hate coming home, because of what it is, and I hate the thought of them having to come home to this. There is nothing to live for because there is no happiness in our lives, nothing to laugh about, just work, work, work, to stay warm and eat as cheaply as we can. In my mind, I wish someone would murder us in our sleep, because I haven't the guts to commit suicide. I have often thought about it. There are easy ways of killing myself but I can't do it. I know my children would be better off if I was to die, and my husband would have no worries then, but I can't do it. I just can't. Please help us, please, you are our last hope now, and if nothing comes of this I shall die, not by committing suicide but of shame and loss of all hope of a new home.' Shelter's message has been one of hope.

The 1974 Community Relations Commission report on *Unemployment and Homelessness* showed how difficult it is to obtain real statistics in areas of human need. It is however clear that the figures for unemployment and homelessness are in general higher than those officially recorded, and that unemployment and homelessness bear considerably more heavily upon the immigrant and coloured population than upon the whites. For boys between the ages of sixteen and twenty for example unemployment among boys born in the West Indies is from two to three times that of the national average for the same age group. The causes for this are various: newness, poverty, discrimination, the failure of English education to make any adjustment to children from a different background. Added to these is sheer disillusion. One social worker made a revealing comment: 'They prefer jobs to be interesting. That is the real difficulty.' It is an indictment of our whole social system. Unemployment in turn adds to the alienation, is closely linked with homelessness, and sometimes leads to lawbreaking.

The record of the churches in Britain in helping the immigrants and their children to be at home is on the whole lamentable. The Community and Race Relations Unit of the British Council of Churches has done some magnificent work, particularly in the resettlement of the Ugandan Asians. Not many churches have been hostile, though there is a record of a Jamaican seeking to attend worship at a church in north London only to be told by the steward at the door that *his* church was further down the road. But for the most part our offences are those of omission rather than of commission. Individuals, particularly educated individuals with a Christian commitment, have been made most welcome. The majority have been treated with indifference. The average Christian does not know how many people there are in his neighbourhood of different ethnic or national backgrounds. He knows nothing about their needs and hopes, their way of life, the difficulties and prejudices they encounter.

Crime too grows where people do not care enough. Dr. Oscar Newman has fascinatingly shown a correlation between crime (including its young brother vandalism) and housing. High-rise apartments, unless the block is occupied solely by the elderly, encourage crime. But it isn't enough of itself to cut the skyscrapers down to size. There must be neighbourliness, so that neighbours observe one another and have a common ground. The nosey neighbour is a defence against crime; the friendly neighbour is a still stronger one.

It is appalling that we in the churches care so little. The parable of the Good Samaritan touches us closely. The priest and Levite passed by on the other side. The Samaritan went straight to the man in need and helped him, thinking nothing of danger, of the diversion of his own immediate purposes, of the prejudices of the man he was seeking to help, or of the cost. But we, consciously or unconsciously, take care not to walk the roads where need may be our neighbour. We seek to avoid the possibility of a challenge. If others thrust the challenge at us we buy it off with a contribution to one of the organisations working where the need lies.

Or we may make a tentative step along the road, and find ourselves rebuffed. What if the Jew says, 'I'm not going to be helped by a dirty Samaritan'? What if the needy says, 'To hell with your middle-class paternalism!'? What if the black thinks we are trying to force him into conformity with our white society? We withdraw, hurt. But our hurtness might arouse in us an uncomfortable suspicion that their words have struck home. Or perhaps we ask a Nigerian round to our house, and he does not come. We have gone to some trouble in preparation. But perhaps he has had a call from his parents, and in his culture respect for his parents and obedience to them takes precedence over everything else. Or perhaps a group of Jamaicans come to our church social; they keep together in a group, and do not take part; the evening is an unqualified flop. Yet they are only behaving in the way the British too often behave abroad. They are no doubt shy, and our very odd recreations are unfamiliar to them. We too seldom make the vital leap of understanding. Even if we are offended there is a great word of Jesus to Peter. 'How often must I forgive my brother if he offends me?' says Peter. 'Seven times?' Seven times? How often have we pressed seven times through rebuffs to our overtures of friendship? 'No,' replied Jesus. 'Seventy times seven.'

The need for caring is very great, and there is here in the first place a programme for our churches. We should be reaching out into the community around us, seeing that our members do go down the streets we never touch, finding out about work conditions and living conditions, drawing new folk, wherever they come from, into the community, knowing where professional help and expert guidance is needed, drawing on the resources of our fellow Christians, not necessarily in our own church, to provide this or to show us where it is to be found, having a regular programme of hospital and prison-visiting, which is not just left to the minister, providing regular visits to the elderly who are living on their own, giving practical help where practical help is needed. Such outreach is part of the very being of a church, and every member except the elderly and infirm should be sharing in it. They too can share in the work. They probably read the local paper more carefully than most and may become aware of needs in that way; they may indeed hear of things by word of mouth which others do not easily find out. And they can share in the constant offering of prayer. Such a church will be the nucleus of a caring community. It will be doing things not for people but with them, sharing with others in common service.

When we come to look at the matter on a world scale our lack of care becomes even clearer. In 1974 Britain generated £1,105 per head of the population; expectation of life was 69. Oil-rich Saudi-Arabia generated £295; expectation of life was 42. Upper Volta generated £26; expectation of life was 26. In north-east Brazil there is one doctor to 5,000 patients; infant mortality is round about 50 per cent, and 60 per cent of the over-fives are illiterate. One of the most telling comments on the way most of mankind live was made by a Muslim woman: 'Allah is very merciful. He gives us food almost every other day.'

The table showing the percentage of the GNP going in Official Development Assistance from some of the wealthier countries is eloquent.

	1960	1972	1975
Australia	0·38	0·59	0·54
Belgium	0·88	0·55	0·62
Canada	0·19	0·47	0·51
France	1·38	0·67	0·51
Italy	0·22	0·09	0·08
Netherlands	0·31	0·67	0·65
Norway	0·11	0·41	0·65
Portugal	1·45	1·79	0·42
UK	0·56	0·39	0·32
USA	0·53	0·29	0·20

The UN target figure is 0·7 per cent. Britain and the USA have both officially stated that they cannot accept this figure; the USA pleaded her 'staggering domestic needs'. Public opinion in Britain is curiously ambivalent. A majority think that we give more to developing countries than we spend on defence; we spend 15 times as much on defence. They think that we give too much to developing countries. But *the same people*, asked what figure it would be right to give, suggested 2½p in the £.

Such a figure would increase our giving by 600 per cent. There is much ignorance to overcome. The Minister of Overseas Development recommends 11p per head per week on overseas aid. The average weekly expenditure per head in Britain on tobacco is 74p and on alcohol £1·30.

Not merely is the assistance too small. Too much of it has strings attached; two thirds of the aid from Britain is tied to the purchase of British goods. Too much is crippling the developing countries with repayment of the interest on loans. The debt is rising at the rate of 14 per cent a year. The flow of prosperity is still from the poorer countries to the richer. The share of the developing countries in total world exports declined between 1938 and 1966 from 30·4 per cent to 19.1 per cent. Within ten years Ghana had to export five times as much cocoa as before in order to pay for a tractor. As René Dumont has pointed out, the total income of the rich countries in 1973 was estimated at about $3,000,000,000,000. The ancient biblical concept was that we should tithe our wealth for the needy. We gave in all, not 10 per cent of that, but 0.005 per cent of it.

In the Far East 100,000 children go blind every year through Vitamin A deficiency. $3 would suffice to save 100 children from blindness. 200 million people suffer from endemic goitre. $1 would save 6 people from this for three years or more. 460,000,000 people are officially declared starving. The USA recently bought 700,000 tonnes of protein – rich fish meal – from Latin America to enrich their cattle and pig feed; it could have satisfied the protein needs of 15,000,000 people for a full year. The rich countries fed 400 million tons of grain and 50 million tons of oil cake to their farm animals in 1973; in the same year human beings were dying of starvation in the Sahel; the grain fed to animals would suffice for the whole population of India and China. The USA spends $20,000,000,000 a year on advertising. A quarter of humanity take home 90 per cent of the world's income, hold 90 per cent of the world's gold reserves, eat 70 per cent of the world's meat and 80 per cent of the world's protein. We are in that quarter.

Statesmen pay lip service to the need. Harold Wilson in Jamaica on 1st May, 1975, declared, 'I want to make it clear in what I propose that my government fully accepts that the relationship, the balance between the rich and poor countries of the world is wrong and must be remedied . . . that the wealth of the world must be redistributed in favour of the poverty-stricken and the starving.' 'I am unable,' said Willy Brandt in 1974, 'to detect any justice in the present system of economic and social relations.' 'The present crisis,' said Giscard D'Estang, 'is an enduring crisis involving a redistribution of the world's resources.' It is hard to see governmental policies which match these fine phrases. Actions would be of more lasting eloquence than words.

If we are to be a caring community, we must think, feel and act on a world-scale. We are one world. We ignore the needs of others at our peril. The words of the busybody neighbour in Terence's play are still apposite: 'I am a human being and I account nothing which affects any human being as foreign to me.'

Yet the problems are overpowering.

The world is so big, and I am so small,
I do not like it, at all, at all.

If we are honest, we all feel sometimes like Robert Louis Stevenson's child.

There are four things we can and should do.

The first is to be well-informed. Everything else depends on that. This means intelligent reading. *The New Internationalist* is by far the best organ of information here; its articles are sometimes one-sided, but only because they are ablaze with a passion to serve those in need. We have tried in *Reconciliation Quarterly* to maintain a steady flow of information and Christian comment related to the Third World. Brigid Fitzgerald's work for UNA has shown a notable combination of knowledge and concern. Third World Publications have put out a number of informed pamphlets on different areas of the world, and on topics such as coffee, bananas, and sugar. And of course there are organisations concerned with fostering knowledge of and friendship with particular countries. There is need for some kind of broad background, but there is much to be said for concentrating on a single country or area, and really becoming intimate with its culture and its needs. For many, such information will be best acquired and shared through a group. Here is another challenge to a church. Should not each member undertake to interest himself in some part of the world, to keep himself informed about it, to maintain contact with a missionary there or with members of the indigenous church, to communicate his knowledge to his fellow church members, and to press for their corporate action and concern when this is needed?

Secondly, for the Christian care means prayer. Such prayer is of little value – though, by God's grace, not of none at all, if it is simply (in other words), 'I wish there weren't so many homeless people in Bangla-Desh,' (perhaps), 'I wish the TV wouldn't keep telling me about homeless people in Bangla-Desh.' As we learn more about Bangla-Desh (for example), through reading, through pictures, through hearing from people who have been there or perhaps are there still, we can enter more fully into their desperate need, we can in thought and prayer become one with them for a moment, we can begin to take a tiny fraction of their burden upon ourselves, and our prayer itself takes wings and leaps out to them, and no one can tell how God may use it. For some the answer to their prayer will come in the form of an action laid upon them. For some older folk their prayer will in itself be the richest service they could offer.

Thirdly, we should not underestimate the value of good, old-fashioned charity. It is no substitute for a juster order. But we have not got a juster order, and while we are hoping for it people are dying. They used to tell a story of the two Pre-Raphaelites, Rossetti and Morris. Confronted with a beggar, Rossetti would empty his pockets and forget about the man. Morris never gave a penny to a beggar, but devoted his life to working for a world in which there would be no beggars. Rossetti was all heart, Morris all head. We need heart and head in harmony. We must help the needy and work for a new order, not either-or but both-and. Jesus is constant in commendation of those who give to the poor: his words speak to us. If $3 will save 100 children from blindness, let us give $3, or $30, or $300 as our resources allow. Let us give wisely. Oxfam and Christian Aid and War on Want have particularly good records in the small proportion of their resources going on administration, and the care with which they choose their projects, alike to meet emergencies, and to help the people in the developing countries to help themselves.

Fourthly, we must be political. Some Christians do not like this; but we have demonstrated that God calls us in society as well as one by one. We may not all be called to join political parties; some do, some don't. But we must be prepared as Christians to write to our MP or to the appropriate Minister of State, just as our concern for those in our immediate vicinity is likely to lead us to draw the attention of the local councillors to the needs we discern, and to go on pestering them, like the importunate widow, until they do something. Further, our action will be more effective if it is corporate. Bodies like the United Nations Association or the Fellowship of Reconciliation exist nationally with the precise purpose of making informed corporate witness to those in authority about *shalom*, peace, including all that affects the well-being and fulfilment of all God's children. And an individual church and a local council of churches can properly make corporate representations, as can the British Council of Churches at a national level and the World Council of Churches internationally.

The things we should press for are relatively simple in the first instance. They are two.

One is that, whatever our internal problems, they are nothing to those faced where people are starving, and that we should promptly raise our Official Development Aid programme to the 0.7 per cent of GNP set as target by the UN, and that this shall be real aid, not loans to be paid back with interest, or gifts tied in to the purchase of products which could be obtained less expensively elsewhere.

The other is effective support for the work of the UN in this field. UN aid is not tied, and it is given in such a way as to encourage local action. In 1975 the UN Development Programme, which supports some 7,000 projects in 141 countries and territories, announced that it was putting major resources into Burma (for a wide variety of purposes), Kenya (mainly for rural development), Kuwait (with priority for industry) and Nigeria (with priority for agriculture). UNDP works *with* not for people. The UNDP total contribution of $1,800,000,000 is outmatched by the recipients' contribution of $2,200,000,000 to the same projects. In the same year, 1975, the UN Industrial Development Organisation adopted a Declaration and Plan of Action by 82 votes to 1 with 7 abstentions. The plan was to increase the share of the developing countries in total world production from 7 per cent to 25 per cent by the end of the century; to eliminate all forms of colonialism and exploitation; to turn UNIDO into a Specialised Agency; to establish an International Development Fund; to eliminate trade barriers; to foster industrialisation, development of infrastructures and small-scale rural industries. The dissentient vote was that of the USA, and the UK was among those abstaining.

We do not care enough.

4

My Father is still working: Work

> But Jesus answered them, 'My Father is working still,
> and I am working.'   John 5.17

A Christian theology of work will start from Jesus's words about
God, 'My Father is still working.' Work is God-given. That we
should work is an aspect of the image of God in which we are
created.

This means that we may not take either of the attitudes which
Christians have sometimes held. We may not say that work is a
curse. This is a generalisation from the story of Adam. In that
story a curse is set, not upon work nor upon the man, but upon
the ground. Something did happen historically, or prehistorically,
to mankind between food-gathering and tillage.

> ... The Father himself willed
> that the path of tillage should not run smoothly, and was the
>   first to turn
> the fields by skill, sharpening our mortal wits with challenges,
> not letting his Kingdom grow listless in lethargy.
>
> (Vergil *Georgics* 1.121–4)

It is a very Toynbean analysis – the challenge, sufficient but not
excessive, to which emergent civilisation responds. But work is
not a punishment for sin. The truth is rather that a fallen world,
a world in which men are free to sin, must also be a world of
hardship. Yet at the same time to face the hardship can be a
calling from God. In the fullness of the Kingdom, God shall wipe
away all tears. In a suffering world, Jesus has shown, for once and
for all, the redemptive power of suffering. To treat work as a

curse is contrary to the truth we have received. It is also the most abject practical folly. To give a schoolchild Shakespeare to learn or a flower bed to dig as a punishment is the surest way to induce him to avoid Shakespeare or gardening like the plague.

Equally dangerous and un-Christian is to see work as irrelevant, and merely a means to a reward. They have a thing in the United States called, shamefully, the Protestant ethic. And indeed, as Max Weber rightly saw, it did arise within the context of Protestant Christianity. Weber's thesis that the change to capitalism in the economic sphere was parallel to *and depended upon* the religious change to Protestantism has been much criticised, both on historical and on theological grounds. But one wonders whether R. H. Tawney's version of it, that Protestantism was providing a religious dress for the new economic order, is not somewhere near the mark. For the so-called Protestant ethic, which justifies the pursuit of profit, and in general adds up to 'Each for himself and the devil – or the dole – take the hindmost', may have something to do with Protestantism but does not seem to have much to do with the ethic of Jesus. For Jesus makes no bones about the possession and pursuit of wealth. It is 'Woe to you rich'. It is impossible to serve God and Mammon. God's world is the world of the parable of the labourers in the vineyard, who do not receive more, the more work they do, or the most skilled they are, but who are equally treated. This is how those who follow Jesus are encouraged to behave, with the supreme impartiality of the weather. 'Why should any Christian *want* to have more money than another?' asked Julius Nyerere. Why indeed?

There is a Christian philosophy, though not a theology, of work, of which this is a caricature. It will be found in one of Paul's letters to Thessalonica.

These are our orders to you, brothers, in the name of our Lord Jesus Christ: hold aloof from every Christian brother who falls into idle habits, and does not follow the tradition you received from us. You know yourself how you ought to copy our example: we were no idlers among you; we did not accept board and lodging from anyone without paying for it; we toiled and drudged, we worked for a living night and day, rather than be a burden to any of you – not because we have not the right to maintenance, but to set an example for you to imitate. For even during our stay with you we laid down the rule: the man who will not work shall not eat. We mention this because we hear that some of your number are idling their time away, minding everybody's business but their own. To all such we give these orders, and we appeal to them in the name of the Lord Jesus to work quietly for their living. (2 Thessalonians 3.6–12)

Behind this lies the immensely sane provision of Jewish education that no child should be pushed out into the world without some practical manual skill, a provision which we might do well to restore in order to redress the balance of our ivory-towered intellectualism.

As a philosophy of work this contains two elements, one positive, one negative. The positive is that those who receive should also give. In the words of Jesus it is a free response to a free gift (Matt. 10.8). Paul is institutionalising it. None the less, it is a sound social philosophy. Bernard Shaw once pointed out that we are all in debt. The moment we step outside our front gate we are using an extremely expensive manufactured article known as a road, and until we have paid scot and lot for this and other ways in which we draw on the resources of the community, we are in debt. We can take a wider view. We are all heirs of the past; we all have a consequent duty to the future.

Negatively, Paul's view is bound up with the human propensity to sin. It can be summed up in the old proverb that Satan finds some mischief still for idle hands to do. The slothful and the sluggard are continually pilloried in the gnomic wisdom of Proverbs, and Paul has inherited something of this. Jesus calls us to positive living: 'He who is not with me is against me, and he who does not gather with me scatters.' (Matt. 12.30). Of course as a philosophy it can have futile applications. Schoolboys and schoolgirls may be given dull tasks of no conceivable educational importance because they are 'work' rather than being allowed or encouraged to follow their own bent. Unemployed people may be set on digging holes and filling them in again, or some equally profitless occupation. Monks may be distracted from more sensual pleasures by being told to copy secular texts: one on a sleepy afternoon produced 'ut ius liberum eosdem dedissent ut ius liberum eosdem dedissent ut ius liberum eosdem dedissent ut ius liberum eosdem dedisse': we may be thankful for the resultant preservation of ancient authors, but that was hardly the object of the exercise. Still, although there is a fullness of place for leisure, as the story of Mary and Martha reminds us, there is a corrupting element in idleness. We return to Toynbee's Christian philosophy of history: it is good to confront a challenge.

A Christian theology of work will contain five elements. First it is a reflection of, even by grace a participation in, the creative and sustaining activity of God. Craftsmanship, in the end, is of the essence of work. This is not a sentimental return to the past such as Morris or Gandhi fostered, though it is as well to be sure that mass-production is the most efficient method available, apart from other values. In the Open University we could hardly cope with our student records were it not for the computer, but it really is more efficient to handpick tutors for summer schools. Even in an age of mass-production there is plenty of room for personal practical skills, as the proliferation of 'do-it-yourself' kits may remind us. Indeed, rising costs are driving many to learn crafts of house-painting, and carpentry, and bread-baking, and wine-making, and bookbinding, and the like. But craftsmanship can work through teams as well as through individuals, and through complex machines as well as simple tools, and the workers in a factory may properly take a creative pride in the products of that factory.

The work of the farmer and market-gardener is in the centre of the mirror. The man who will not work shall not eat, perhaps. But the man who does not eat cannot work. The sophistication of modern technology has removed many of us, too many of us, away from the earth. We are more familiar with macadam and concrete than we are with earth and grass, and the shoelessness of the young, apart from being better for the feet, and much better than platform-shoes or stiletto heels, is a healthy return to contact with the soil. Any people depend on their agriculture; in a sound economy it will rank first, for all else derives from adequate food. Some of the most solid gains in the Chinese revolution spring from a stress on agriculture.

The sustaining activity is equally important. Some activities are so remote from the coal-face (to use the fashionable cliché) that it is hard to see their relevance, and some may in fact be irrelevant and have come into being through a branch of Parkinson's Law. Even in a simpler age not everyone was creatively active. There may be dubious politicians and too many civil servants, but politicians and civil servants of some sort, shape and size are probably necessary to the sustaining activities of the Lord in the twentieth century. There can be as much pride for all concerned, from porters down to the traffic-controller, in running trains to time as in any creative process. Skilled chairmanship and computer-programming alike are of the Lord. So is cleaning the office.

> All may of thee partake:
> Nothing can be so mean,
> Which with this tincture (for thy sake)
> Will not grow bright and clean.
>
> A servant with this clause
> Makes drudgerie divine
> Who sweeps a room, as for Thy laws,
> Makes that and th' action fine.
> (George Herbert *The Elixir*)

Secondly, work is service. The Christian is called to serve. The Son of Man came not to be served but to serve. Work should be useful. Work is an aspect of membership of the community. In a

48

simple society the necessary tasks would be identified and apportioned. In a complex society this cannot be directly achieved. None the less, there is something wrong if people feel that their work is of no importance to God or man. In the end the unpleasant but socially necessary tasks have to be seen as part of the service of the community, though some of the sting can be taken out of them by the effective use of machines. A Greek comic dramatist by a fine flight of invention envisaged a world in which automation takes the place of slavery:

> The stuff'll come
> when you call it. 'Table, attention!
> Now lay yourself. Trough, knead the dough.
> Jug, pour. Where's that cup? Off with you and
> wash yourself up.
> Cake, up you get. Why hasn't that bowl served the
> beetroot?
> Fish, here!' 'But I'm not yet done on the other side.'
> 'All right, turn over, and sprinkle yourself with oil and
> salt.'
>
> (Crates)

It could take the place of some of the uglier aspects of wage-slavery. But most people will do a grinding task with relative cheerfulness if they can see something coming of it in the end.

Thirdly, work should where possible spring from and be related to an individual's own talents and natural aptitudes. Further, the individual should be regarded as a person, not as a stereotype: it is not easy for most women in Britain to find employment except as teachers, secretaries, nurses and shop-assistants, because this is their stereotype, despite the fact that in some countries they have shown themselves ourstanding doctors and engineers. To seek to relate work to aptitude is not just bourgeois romanticism. It is only applying on a larger scale what is done in a *kibbutz*. In Christian terms it is the application to the body politic of Pauline teaching about the body ecclesiastic.

But each of us has been given his gift, his due portion of

49

Christ's bounty ... And these were his gifts: some to be apostles, some prophets, some evangelists, some pastors and teachers, to equip God's people for work in his service, to the building up of the body of Christ. (Ephesians 4.7–12 NEB)

This is magnificently developed in the first letter to Corinth (1 Cor. 12) where Paul shows how the varieties of gifts lead to varieties of service and varieties of work, yet all derived from a single source and operating in a single community for a single purpose. So comes the elaborate image of the church as the Body of Christ, and we its several members, each with our peculiar function, complementary to that of others. But this also is true of society at large. We are not being merely punnish if we treat Christ's parable of the talents as applying to our natural gifts. Part of the point of the parable is sometimes missed. It is those of us with the lesser gifts who are most likely to be guilty of failing to develop them. To take an image from university life, the first-class honours man gets his first more often than not. But there are many, many thirds who could get seconds if they tried. Abraham Flexner complained that the American universities were turning out second-rate book-keepers. If book-keeping is a necessary social function they had better be second-rate than third-rate.

Fourthly, Christianity is an incarnational religion and is not afraid of the world of matter. The eternal Word of God put on a material body. It is Manichean not Christian, Gnostic not Christian, Platonist not Christian, to run away from solid, toil-some, tiresome contact with the world of matter. If our Master's hands were rough and calloused with the use of saw and plane, we should be proud to earn blistered hands and aching muscles in useful manual work. In the mid-1970s, as the universities could no longer afford to expand, and fewer teachers were needed in the schools, graduates, sometimes with Ph.D.s, were found doing manual work. Why, in Heaven's name, not? The shame is that too few of them were willing to soil their hands. Granted our last point, that those with intellectual training are best employed where they can use their trained talents, it is still better for them to do something useful than to do nothing. People are crying out for help in gardens. It is impossible to find people to help with repairs in the house which require a little more skill than the average husband or wife possesses, but a skill which would be reasonably easily acquired by someone who put his mind to it. It is ridiculous that people should be drifting round grumbling that they have nothing to do, when all they mean is that they are not prepared to do the work which needs doing. (Of course the unemployed and the jobs are not always in the same area. But sometimes they are.) There is a story told of Albert Schweitzer, paternalistic and out-of-date though many of his attitudes were. He, revolutionary theologian, leading Bach scholar and exponent, trained in medicine to repay a little of the debt Europe owes to Africa. He was building his hospital in Lambarene, and asked a passing African if he would lend a hand with carrying some planks across the compound. 'I don't carry planks,' said the African. 'I'm an intellectual.' 'I congratulate you,' said Schweitzer, shouldering the planks. 'I'd always hope to be one myself.' The disease of misobanausia is not confined to African intellectuals.

Fifthly, there is a personal side to all work. There is some tendency to divide occupations and avocations into two, according as they deal with things or people, or perhaps three, ideas, things and people. There is no doubt truth in this. But we cannot escape the personal in anything we do. A bus-conductor is there to perform a simple exchange of a piece of paper for a sum of money, but we all know how much difference his tact and cheerfulness can make to those travelling. Bad blood between workers in a factory can have an extremely adverse effect on that factory's productivity. Even the most mechanical tasks will need something like Christian love brooding over them and operating through them.

There are some cold, hard, practical conclusions to be drawn from this theology of work.

First, socially necessary work should be encouraged and socially useless work discouraged. This can in the end be done only by governmental action, direct or indirect. It is preposterous that at a time of acute inflation the advertising industry, which by definition is seeking to induce customers to buy that which they would not otherwise buy, should be one of the largest in the country. It is preposterous that the National Health Service should be dependent on doctors from the Third World, who are needed in their own homelands.

Secondly, it is important that all workers can relate their particular task to a complete achievement. One of the most exciting changes in recent years has been the Volvo experiment in doing away with the assembly-line so that workers can identify themselves with a complete car and not just a single component. It is more extravagant in factory lay-out but more satisfying to those participating.

Thirdly, teamwork is important. It was discovered in Sweden that piecework payment caused industrial unrest; its abolition reduced unrest but also reduced productivity. But total productivity bonuses increased productivity without increasing unrest, seemingly because they were not competitive.

Fourthly, individual fulfilment through peculiar skills is important. Another Swedish discovery was that representation of workers on boards of management did not help managerial decisions or allay discontent. But the use of workers' councils to isolate and solve problems on the factory floor proved triumphantly successful, and one great shipbuilding firm has left the metalworkers' union to deal with all labour problems. In this way people are being encouraged to do that which they are best qualified to do.

Fifthly, there really should be no unemployment. Today the community properly recognises our responsibility to give all its members an adequate standard of living whether or not they are employed, though we have come near to failing in this with old age pensioners. If this is so, it is ridiculous that the community should not be receiving service in return. The unemployed teenager, with his sense of being unwanted, provides a major social problem which should never have been allowed to arise. Much more far-seeing, flexible planning is needed, so that in any area there is always useful work to be performed.

Sixthly, there is a great deal to be said for sharing out the really unpleasant, unskilled jobs among the whole community in exactly the same way that fire-watching duties were allocated during the war. It would do neither us nor our jobs any harm if we went round with the dust carts for one morning each quarter.

Seventhly, differential rewards ought to be reduced. A dustman is, after all, doing as important a job in his own way as a doctor; the doctor heals disease, but the dustman prevents it. 'Ah, but the doctor has to be compensated for his long unearning period of training.' There is a simple answer to this. All tertiary students should see their higher education as the beginning of their service to the community; they should receive a salary, not a grant; then there would be no catching up to do.

'Commit your work to God,' says the book of Proverbs (16.3). 'The dignity of work' is no mere catchphrase; it is a Christian truth. To reject it, explicitly or implicitly, is to fall below the practical insight of Paul's pagan contemporary Musonius Rufus. Musonius, who belonged to the Cynic wing of Stoicism, castigated those students who regarded themselves as above manual work. He was not ashamed to be seen doing forced labour (a punishment for alienated intellectuals under Nero) on the projected Corinth canal. 'You're distressed to see me helping Greece by digging through this neck of land, are you? Well, what would you have felt like if you'd seen me making a public exhibition of myself on the harp, like Nero?' It is a characteristic answer. Honest manual labour is better than pretension to aestheticism, especially when the work itself is of service. Musonius particularly approves of agriculture. It is natural to till the earth for sustenance, and it does not matter whether you are working on your own land or an employee of another man. Sowing and reaping and threshing corn, planting and cultivating trees, being a shepherd – these are in the full sense liberal occupations. The best form of higher education, says Musonius, would be to work in the fields alongside your professor.

So the Christian dramatist, Dorothy L. Sayers in *The Zeal of Thy House* lets Raphael defend William of Sens, builder of Canterbury:

> Behold he prayeth; not with the lips alone,
> But with the hand and with the cunning brain
> Men worship the Eternal Architect.
> So, when the mouth is dumb, the work shall speak
> And save the workman. True as mason's rule
> And line can make them, the shafted columns rise
> Singing like music; and by day and night
> The unsleeping arches with perpetual voice
> Proclaim in Heaven, to labour is to pray.

So the Nigerian Christian journalist, Gabriel Ojo, has written that the Yoruba greeting *E ku 'se Oluwa O*, given to pastors for doing God's work, should be given to roadmenders, nurses and houseboys – not to mention wives. *Laborare est orare*. Work is prayer.

5

The earth is the Lord's: Conservation

> The earth is the Lord's and the fullness thereof; the world, and those who dwell therein:
>
> for he has founded it upon the seas, and established it upon the rivers.
>
> Psalm 24, 1–2

Loren Eisley in *The Firmament of Time* tells the story of one of the devisers of the atomic bomb coming upon a small tortoise in the woods. He picked it up to take home to his children, then suddenly looked doubtful, retraced his steps, and replaced the tortoise on the spot from which he had taken it. A friend with him watched with surprise. The physicist turned to his friend and remarked, 'It just struck me that perhaps, for one man, I have tampered enough with the Universe.'

In the book of Genesis God looks at everything that he has made, and finds it very good. More, he puts man into the garden of Eden to till it and care for it. He takes man as his partner in the work of creation with a share in the naming of animals, and provides the animals to be companions for man. The earth is the Lord's, and man is God's vice-regent to look after it. This is man's peculiar stewardship, and he has exercised his stewardship unjustly, and, like the unjust steward in the parable, he had better make haste to do recompense to the earth he has abused and the nature he has assaulted.

'Christianity,' said Max Nicholson in *The Environmental Revolution*, 'has signally failed to bear witness to its indebtedness, and to teach the need for respect and reverence towards what it professes to regard as the works of the Creator.' Christianity is an abstraction; it were better to say that Christians have so failed.

The first step must be plainly to reject and to scrub out the complacent image of Man the Conqueror of Nature, and of Man Licenced by God to conduct himself as the earth's worst pest. An intensive spell of environmental repentance is called for, coupled with frank recognition that mankind must finally and unequivocally renounce all claims to be above ecological laws . . . [there is need for] a thorough theological rethinking and restatement of the appropriate standards of responsibility, but this the churches have abysmally failed to undertake . . . Only during the past few years, under pressure from outside, have there been any signs within the churches of interest in evaluating and reviving vital elements in Christian tradition which have been increasingly neglected since the days of St. Francis of Assisi.

Man's inhumanity to nature can be broadly analysed under two heads – pollution and exhaustion. In 1901 Dean Hole in his autobiographical *Then and Now*, welcoming the new laws on sanitary inspection, wrote:

There is even hope, although at present it is little more than a glow-worm in a wood, a good deed in a naughty world, but the time may come when the abomination of desolation itself . . . the noxious fumes and vapours of smoke, which pollute our atmosphere and darken out light, may hurt the earth no more; when no man shall imperil or impair the breath of their fellows to satisfy the greed of gain; when the children of those now dwarfed and pale shall regain the stature and the glow of health; when the fish shall swim in the pure stream, and the white sheep shall graze on the green pastures, and the thrush shall sing amid the blossoms of the orchard, and the garden shall be gay with flowers.

Three quarters of a century later we are still reading of dead fish floating on rivers polluted with industrial waste, of birds poisoned by consuming insects affected by insecticides, of flowers withering in the hedgerows, and the very hedgerows cut down and uprooted. We need, as Kenneth Mellanby has put it, air fit for lichens and water fit for fish. Man's own condition is ironical. As Tom Lehrer, the Harvard humorist, has it:

Pollution! Pollution! You can use the latest toothpaste,
And rinse out your mouth with industrial waste.

Our society has become the effluent society. The longest sewer in Europe is the Rhine. Each day it carries into the Netherlands 31,800 metric tons of chloride; 14,000 tons of sulphates; 9,700 tons of calcium; 3,443 tons of magnesium; 2,000 tons of nitrates. It all begins with the industrial waste of Basel. The French of Alsace add the salt which makes the water brackish. The West Germans pump in, untreated, 29 per cent of all their industrial waste. The Dutch grumble, and add to the pollution. The river Mersey receives 52,000,000 gallons of trade effluent a day; one report has described it also as a 'massive unflushed lavatory'. In the USA, at Fitchburg, Mass., there is a standard joke that the greatest fire hazard is the river, and that there should be NO SMOKING notices on the bridges. It is no joke: the river Cuyahoga in Cleveland, Ohio, did catch fire. If Jesus walked the water today he would have to contend with oilslick, boards, bottles and industrial waste of all kinds.

In the cities the problem of pollution has become peculiarly acute. In Tokyo they actually have street-corner machines in which you insert a coin to secure a whiff of fresh air. Despite much recent legislation the cities remain filthy, the air remains noxious, and the noise level is not less damaging because it is taken for granted. Tom Lehrer again puts it pungently:

Living in the cities is quite a thrill.
If the hoods don't get you, the monoxide will.

Los Angeles has been a standard lesson how not to live. It is in a marvellous situation, set in a basin among the mountains. But I have heard it said that 40 per cent of the basin is a network of roads, and the unburned hydrocarbons from the automobiles turn the blue sky into a pall of smog perpetually enveloping the city. Lewis Mumford called these palaeotechnic paradises by the expressive name of Coketown. The ingredients of their industrially produced atmosphere included chlorine, ammonia, carbon monoxide, phosphoric acid, fluorine, methane, not to mention some two hundred cancer-producing chemicals, often in stagnant lethal concentrations. Even in 1952, in one week, 5,000 Londoners died of such a concentration of lethal gases.

Warnings about the exhaustion of the earth's resources have been appearing regularly across the past thirty years. At first they were voices crying in the wilderness. As I write I have in front of me three books published a quarter of a century ago. At the time few people attended to them. In 1948 Fairfield Osborn wrote a book with the already significant title *Our Plundered Planet*. In prologue he wrote these words.

> Nature may be a thing of beauty and is indeed a symphony, but above and below and within its own immutable essences, its distances, its apparent quietness and changelessness it is an active, purposeful, co-ordinated machine. Each part is dependent upon another, all are related to the movement of the whole. Forests, grasslands, soils, water, animal life – without one of these the earth will die – will become dead as the month. This is provable beyond questioning. Parts of the earth, once living and productive, have thus died at the hand of man. Others are now dying. If we cause more to die, nature will compensate for this in her own way, inexorably, as already she has begun to do.

He proceeded to draw attention, first to the fact that the population of the world had multiplied five times in the previous three centuries (a quarter of a century later it is nearly double his figure); then that two-thirds of the people were living in three populous areas of Europe, China–Japan, India–Ceylon, in about one eighth of the land surface; that man-made eroision was losing the fertile topsoil; that DDT was damaging the life-pattern;

and that man was generally destructive of other animals, as with the reduction of the North American bison within a century from 50,000,000 to 500. The problems, though recently aggravated, are not new: deforestation and erosion can be traced back to the ancient world. But the immense proliferation of human beings makes them urgent to solve.

In the same year William Vogt published *Road to Survival*. 'Despoiled forests, erosion, wildlife extermination, overgrazing, and the dropping of water tables are unforeseen and unwanted by-blows of a vigorous and adolescent culture on the loose.' Vogt shows that profits are loss, that in fifty years the New England shad catch dropped to one fifth of its previous level, that the sardine catch in California dropped to one half in five years, that in a century the guano resources of Peru were reduced from 23,000,000 tons to 30,000 tons, all through the pursuit of quick and large profit without thought for the future. The land is supersaturated and in an ecological sense the books do not balance. Vogt pricks a number of economic bubbles and examines carefully with tables and diagrams the pattern of ecological stability. The most damaging impact of 'civilised' man on his environment is the shattering of the hydrologic cycle. This may reduce the amount of water that falls; it does certainly reduce the amount available to man; the prime cause is destruction of the plant cover. We cannot force land into the pattern we wish to impose upon it, but must fit the use to the land, its capabilities and its limitations. From this point Vogt moves on to some telling comparisons between the standard of living in different parts of the world, leading to the overall conclusion that man has moved into an untenable position by protracted and wholesale violation of certain natural laws; to re-establish himself he must bring his behaviour into conformity with natural limitations. In effect this means that renewable resources should be used to produce as much wealth as possible *on a sustained-yield basis*; that we should, therefore, adjust out demand to the supply, either by consuming less per person or by maintaining fewer people.

The third, and most depressed, of the books was written at the same time, but owing to the author's death in 1948 not published till 1951. This is *The Estate of Man* by the poet, mathematician and philosopher, Michael Roberts. Roberts starts from the fact that the population is increasing and the food-yielding area diminishing. If the earth's land surface were parcelled out between its (then) 2,350,000,000 people, each would have 15 acres, 5 of jungle or forest, 4 of desert, 2 of near-desert, 2 of snow, and 2 potentially fertile (about $1\frac{1}{2}$ under cultivation). It takes 3 acres to supply a citizen of the UK with his food. Roberts argues urgently the damage done by erosion. He then passes to sources of energy, and writes 'The world has enough oil to last for twenty-two years,' – this was an underestimate, but it was a salutary shock – 'enough coal to last five hundred, and enough damsilliness to last for ever.' There are other sources of energy available, through water and nuclear power and, potentially through the interior heat of the earth, the sun's radiation and the tides, but it would require an immense use of energy from other sources to develop them. Roberts also said some searching things about our failure to use the natural gifts of humanity to the full, or to have any reservoir of talent. His attitude would today be called élitist, but his questions remain relevant. The work was unfinished at his death. He planned his final chapters in which he identified war as the greatest of all wasters of resources. We must return to harmony with nature and so to harmony with our neighbours; war springs from disequilibrium. To return to a harmonious relation with the soil would be a spiritual as well as a material advance.

The most pessimistic of these verdicts has not been fulfilled, but the need for a responsible husbanding of resources remains as strong as ever.

Alongside pollution and exhaustion there is the effect on ecology of some of man's well-meant endeavours to improve his economic condition. This has been spelt out with a rare combination of knowledge and emotion, science and eloquence, by Rachel Carson in *Silent Spring*. The simple fact is that weedkillers and insecticides, which have proliferated indiscriminately since the second World War, have come to endanger all life, human life included. DDT is a widely familiar insecticide. Individuals with no known exposure to it, except from eating food which has been grown with its help, may absorb a damaging level of it, farm workers 3 times as much, and chemical workers 100 times as much. Parathion, used by the millions of pounds in the USA alone, was causing an average of over 300 deaths a year in Japan in the early 1960s. It seems that there is a growing danger of cancer through drinking water contaminated by pesticides.

An excellent example of wider ecological damage is reported from Wyoming. In an area dominated by sage there was exciting wild life. Willows grew along the banks of streams and creeks. Moose and beaver fed on the willows. The beavers dammed the streams with the willows they felled, and in the lake thus formed the trout and waterfowl flourished. To extend the grasslands for the cattle-ranchers the area was sprayed to destroy the sage. The chemical used destroyed the willows with the sage. The moose vanished. The beaver vanished. The dam collapsed. The lake drained away. The trout shrunk to a few inches. 'The living world was shattered. When poisons were used against Japanese beetle in the USA, birds died by the hundreds, and thousands, squirrels died, cats and dogs died, earthworms died, and some sheep died.' Lord Shackleton in his introduction to Rachel Carson's book told of 6,000 birds dead on a single estate at Tumby in Lincolnshire in the spring of 1961 through indiscriminate spraying, and the fertility of those birds which survived was gravely affected. One recalls the story of Spike Milligan taking part in a service in St. Paul's on the theme of conservation. He read the passage 'the wolf also shall dwell with the lamb, and the leopard shall lie down with the kid; and the calf and the young lion and the fatling together ... and the lion shall eat straw like the ox', and added, 'And I would like to add, the wolf, the leopard and the lion are now extinct in biblical lands, so let us draw a lesson from that Lesson.'

In the early 1970s concern for the environment came to much greater prominence. 1972 was a key year. January saw *The Ecologist* publish *A Blue-Print for Survival*. The tenor of this hard-hitting paper was that 'the principal defect of the industrial way of life with its ethos of expansion is that it is not sustainable'; only a social revolution, which must include taxation to help to control resources, decentralisation of power and a return to smaller communities, can solve our environmental and ecological problems. In March Dennis Meadows and a group of his colleagues produced a volume on behalf of the so-called Club of Rome entitled *The Limits of Growth*. They show that if the expansion of industry continues at its present rate, non-renewable natural resources will be exhausted within a century and the food supply will become inadequate; that there is grave danger anyway to the food-supply from pollution, even if fresh sources of power are discovered; that even if this is controlled, the growth of population will outstrip the food-supply; and that the combination of all three, even in a modified form, will lead to the collapse of the human system of living within about a hundred years. To achieve equilibrium we must now simultaneously check the growth of population, the expansion of industry, and pollution, and before long, food production. Then in June came the Stockholm Conference on the Environment. It arose from a deep concern about imminent disaster. One of the deepest anxieties was over water. (It is worth remembering that the greatest achievement of the Romans was to bring water to the people. In some parts of north Africa and the near east fertility has been restored to the fields by opening up the clogged water-channels constructed by the Romans. Roman baths were regarded as luxurious by moralists of the day. But, as John Wesley put it, cleanliness is after all next to godliness.) Maurice Strong, Secretary-General of the Conference stated: 'The environmental crisis has made us aware that the future life and well-being of man depends upon the preservation of a healthy equilibrium in the natural systems which provide the essential ingredients for his life – water, air, soil, plant and animal life. These systems are a fragile, finite and interdependent part of the complex unitary system of inter-acting relationships which embrace the entire globe.' In the event the conclusions of the conference were surprisingly cautious, though one important practical effect was a Convention against Ocean Dumping. At the same time an independent body concerned with the environment, named Dai Dong, came up with a more radical statement. In sum:

1. Human beings inhabit the earth, but not they alone.
2. There is a fundamental conflict between traditional concepts of economic growth and the preservation of the environment.
3. Exploitation by foreign corporations has led to economic disparity.
4. Population growth cannot continue indefinitely with finite resources, but this problem is not to be seen in isolation.
5. Economic development of any kind will require technology.
6. The culture of the industrial nations, based on an accumulation of material goods, stands in the way of rational solutions.
7. Among the most critical problems that constitute a threat to human survival is war.

Three years later came a second report to the Club of Rome, by Mihajlo Mesarovic and Eduard Pestel. It is somewhat less pessimistic than the first. It repeats the lesson of the first, that our problems derive from our obsession with Bigness and Growth. The current crises, according to Mesarovic and Pestel, are not temporary, but represent a persistent trend. Only global solutions will do; this means a new world economic order; traditional economic theory is inadequate; all the disciplines concerned with ecology must work together. But, this said, the crises can be resolved by co-operation. This means planning for the distant future; breaking down our narrowing national-isms; constructing an effective international framework. It means prompt action; reverence for the world around us; practical love for those in distress. For the individual it demands enlarging his outlook into world consciousness; a new ethic in the use of material resources, saving and conserving rather than spending and discarding; the realisation that he is part of nature, and a search for harmony with nature rather than conquest of nature; a sense of identification with future generations.

Growth of population represents one of the most serious inroads into the balance of nature. In 1970 the population of the world was 3,632,000,000. It is growing each year by more than the total population of Britain. At the present rate of increase it will reach 6,494,000,000 in AD 2000. In those thirty years the less developed regions will rise by more than a third. There is no significant part of the world where the population is declining or even stable. The areas of the largest expansion are Middle and Latin America, southern Asia, north Africa, and Polynesia. Yet already between 10 and 20 million die of malnutrition each year. If each couple limited their family to two children it would be 70 years before the population ceased to increase; yet people go on wanting more children than the world can support. If the growth of population is not checked, disaster lies ahead, and any parents who seek more than two children should first weigh very, very carefully and prayerfully, what they are about. At the same time it is vital to raise standards of living throughout the world, for it has been amply shown that as the standard of living rises above the borderline of misery the population growth has a tendency to be reduced. We must reverse the vicious circle, and make a virtuous circle of it. As Paul Ehrlich has put it in *The World's Children*, to save the children there must be fewer of them. Or, to put it differently, there can be no death control without birth control.

This destruction of God's world and its resources is totally alien to the insights of scripture. Two great passages might almost form a programme for us, one from the Old Testament, one from the New. The first proclaims:

Then I will make a covenant on behalf of Israel with the wild beasts, the birds of the air, and the things that creep on the earth, and I will break bow and sword and weapon of war and

64

sweep them off the earth, so that all living creatures may lie down without fear. (Hosea 2.18)

The other enjoins: Do no damage to sea or land or trees. (Revelation 7.3)

When we add to these Jesus's manifest delight in the flowers of the field (Matt. 6.28) and his declaration of God's care for the fall of a sparrow (Matt. 10.29) we glimpse something of the condemnation under which we stand. The sparrow which finds a house and the swallow which builds a nest in the altars of the Lord (the passage is so familiar that we do not realise just how startling it is) stand in stark contrast to the poisoned birds around us.

We can draw some conclusions.

First, the need for humility. Our scientific advances, which should lead us to humility before the wonders of the universe they reveal, sometimes produce the sort of arrogance which assumes that we know all the answers. In fact the very methods of science, which thrives by the isolation of problems, make it a very dangerous instrument for use in the natural world, where problems are never found in isolation. Dr. J. Briejer, the admirable Director of the Plant Protection Service in the Netherlands, put this forcefully.

> The resort to weapons such as insecticides to control it [life] is a proof of insufficient knowledge and of an incapacity so to guide the processes of nature that brute force becomes unnecessary. Humbleness is in order; there is no excuse for scientific conceit here.

Only he who humbles himself shall be exalted. Only he who humbles himself is fitted to inherit the earth. So let us be healthily sceptical about our technological achievements. A moratorium on technical innovation might do no harm. The American farmer who said, 'What's the use of trying to make me farm better? I don't farm as well as I know how at the moment!' was a wise man. If organic farming and gardening can deliver the goods without artificial fertilisers and insecticides, let us practise them, for God's sake and for the sake of his world. And if not, let us be modest in experiment, till we know the full consequences.

Second, reverence for life: Schweitzer's phrase expresses it well. Dr. Briejer is again relevant: 'Life is a miracle beyond our comprehension, and we should reverence it even where we have to struggle against it.' Even if we do not feel called to go all the way with the Jains in their practice of *ahimsa* or 'non-harming' towards all living creatures, so that they veil their very breath for fear or damaging the tiny insect-life of the air, yet we should not needlessly and carelessly destroy life. How can we claim to be disciples of that Jesus who declared that his Father cared even for the fall of a sparrow, and accept the destruction of thousands of sparrows through the ignorant use of insecticides? We shall not destroy rare species unless, like the smallpox virus, they are killers with few redeeming features – and even then we need to be humble. We may use forests for charcoal, or ship-building, or paper, but let us replace what we take.

Third, we must exercise our power responsibly. I know of no one who has put this better than Rev. Harold O. Wilson of Athol, Mass.:

As we 'tamper' with the universe we have discovered that it is necessary to destroy in order to create. In fact there is not creation without destruction of some kind. The marble must yield to the blows of the sculptor. The earth must be torn by the plow. The pigment must be crushed by the painter. The wood must be ripped by the carpenter. The truth is that life is given for life. But it seems that in our ingenuity we have managed to reverse this process. We create in order to destroy. In fact one shudders to think how we have abused our trust of the universe. We create in order to destroy our natural environment. We create in order to destroy our created environment. The urban sprawl represents more and more a tangle hostile to human life. We create in order to destroy our social environment. The exploitation and mistrust we live by threatens to send us up in one magnificent conflagration.

There is all the difference in the world between responsible use and irresponsible exploitation. Monetary profit is here the most blinding of all motives. The sense that we would have no power if it did not come from the God who created all these things offers a truer direction.

Fourth, because we are members of society and because God is the Lord of that society there are pressures which we can and should bring on these in society. When it was proposed to flood a unique ecological area in Upper Teesdale, because the ICI plant lower down needed more water, it was not easy to balance the conflicting interests. But it was entirely proper and essential to ensure that the values which were not merely economic should be laid sharply before the Government. René Dumont, that admirable gadfly, has proposed the use of taxation to check wastefulness. Two of his proposals are surely worth pursuing further. One is a durability tax on all products, directed against built-in obsolescence, 100 per cent on products lasting less than a year, and nil on those lasting 100 years. The other is a progressive tax on water and electricity, designed to penalise excess. Recycling needs wider public encouragement, including the selective collection of refuse, so that material for recycling is separate. We can press for more research into alternative sources of energy. Sir George Porter has said with sad truth, 'If sunbeams were weapons, solar energy would have been developed long ago.'

Finally, there are things which we can do ourselves severally and individually. One excellent church in Minneapolis invites all those round about to deposit their unwanted material in the basement. One of their church members, a genius with his hands, turns broken throwaway material into serviceable objects again; the basement is thronged after school hours with children learning how to make toys and decorations out of the most improbable junk, so that they too are acquiring constructive and creative leisure activities. Or less demonstratively, we can simply

67

deal with our own rubbish sensibly, collect milk bottle tops, put a brick in the lavatory cistern to use less water, avoid litter and speak a word in season to litter-louts, switch off lights which are not in use, limit our families, and avoid the unnecessary use of motor cars. For care of God's world, like charity, begins at home.

6

Not by might: Decentralisation

Not by might, nor by power, but by my Spirit, says the Lord of Hosts.

Zechariah 4.6

'Power tends to corrupt, and absolute power corrupts absolutely.' So said the Christian historian, Lord Acton, in one of the most misquoted sentences in the English language. It gives one cardinal reason why the Christian should foster decentralisation. Man is not to be trusted with too much power. In the modern world there has to be centralised planning. The world is hungry, individuals can do something to alleviate that hunger, but the problems of world hunger will be solved only by intergovernmental action on a massive scale. National economic problems require national action. Some kind of a national health service is a necessity. Here again, disease knows no political boundaries, and concern for the sick elsewhere and enlightened self-interest alike leads us to concerted action through the World Health Organisation for the elimination of the diseases that prey upon mankind. Wendell Willkie's 'one world' is in some senses an ineluctable fact. People are already speaking of 'the global village'. But the more that power is concentrated, the more dangerous it becomes. It is essential that it is countered by the checks and balances of a genuinely local sense of responsibility.

Secondly, we seek a society in which the individual counts. This too is part of our Christian insight. The Archbishop of Canterbury in his Call to the Nation in October 1975 reassured individuals that they count. They count in the sight of God. But in the sight of Man? Dr. Coggan was specific: 'Your vote counts.'

69

But it is not true, not in any normal sense. Psephology has become a somewhat noisy science. We now know that the swing in almost any election is going to depend on something like 10 per cent of the constituencies. It can hardly be described as a deeply democratic privilege to cast a vote once every four or five years for a candidate who in the vast majority of constituencies is either a sure winner or a hopeless case. It is of course not democratic at all, in any sense that the ancient Greeks, who invented the word, would have understood. They would have called our political system not a democracy, but an elective aristocracy. And if direct democracy is impracticable in an organisation as large as the modern nation-state, we need to look at the values in a true democracy and see how we can incorporate them. There is in fact a historical irony about the growth of 'democracy' in the nineteenth century. I read in a biography of Lord Rosebery, the Victorian statesman: 'It had come to be realised that the more the franchise was enlarged the less the electorate had any real power to influence policy, the less Parliament represented the nation, and the less Government respected Parliament.'

Christians believe in what George Fox called 'that of God in every man'. Administrative skills, knowledge of financial or foreign affairs, oratorical eloquence may be stronger in one person than in another, but they are not synonymous with sound judgement about the affairs of the community. Wisdom is not coterminous with knowledge. Of course, there are ways in which the individual does count. The individuals who switch off unnecessary lights are genuinely contributing to conservation of energy, the individuals who restrain themselves from luxury buying are private soldiers in the front line of the war against inflation, the individuals who give generously to Oxfam or Christian Aid are saving lives, the individuals who refuse to move from their house when a coloured family moves in next door but find themselves enriched by wider horizons, all count. But our political institutions do not encourage them.

For the Christian who has learned something of the love of

neighbour through God's love for himself, will seek the full development, the *shalom* or wholeness of each of his fellows. And that will surely be achieved only through a happy home-life, useful work, enjoyable recreation, and membership of a community. It is the fulfilment of the vision of the people of God living in secure peace, each under his vine and fig-tree (1 Kings 4.25; Zech. 3.10), and calling every man his neighbour.

Thirdly, there are pragmatic reasons for decentralisation, and Christians, who hold a doctrine of the Incarnation, should also see in a solid pragmatism the hand of the Lord.

One is a lesson to be learned from history: the cynic who observed that the only lesson to be learned from history is that nobody ever learns any lesson from history is not to be followed! It is a frightening fact that the Roman Empire gave to a larger area of the globe a longer period of untroubled peace than at any time in the history of man either before or since, save perhaps for some epochs in China. Rome conquered as a ruthless military autocracy. But she did not so govern. The whole of North Africa, from the borders of Egypt to the Atlantic, was policed by a single legion, nominally 6,000 men but invariably under strength, though with some auxiliary support. When we reflect that this vast area includes as a small part the Kabylie where in recent years determined guerrillas were able to fight off the power of France it is clear that, however Rome conquered, she ruled with the consent of the governed. The secret of this lay partly in Rome's immense capacity to absorb the peoples she ruled. Roman settlers did not form a class apart, but intermingled freely with those among whom they settled. Already in the first century BC the key figures in Latin literature were from 'Gaul south of the Alps'; in the first century AD they were from Spain; by AD 200 from Africa. But more important still was the strength of the *municipium*, the township, fostered by Roman imperial policy. Such townships might be to all intents and purposes self-governing, except that they might not make war. The Romans believed in an intense local loyalty, a local sense of community, of 'belonging'. Alongside this they encouraged a commitment to Rome. Roman citizenship was at first the reward of the privileged few for loyalty and service. By the early third century AD virtually every citizen of any township within the empire had been enrolled as a citizen of Rome. What the Romans sought to destroy were the intermediate loyalties. Nationalism, as we understand it, they regarded as divisive and disruptive. After the story of the past five centuries in Europe it is hard to think that they are wrong. The immeasurable majesty of the Roman peace depended on strong local attachments, on an effective decentralisation going along with a strong central government.

We may link with this the increasingly important concept of optimum size. We have tended to pursue the maximum. But optimum and maximum are not the same. Unfortunately it seems impossible to determine optimum size until you have passed it. There seemed no reason why airports should not go on expanding – until O'Hare (Chicago) and J. F. Kennedy (New York) became clogged up: they had passed their optimum size in pursuit of the maximum. There seemed no reason why universities should not go on expanding – until the huge campuses of the USA and France exploded in unrest and it became clear that the individual had been swamped in the mass and was reasserting himself. Those who teach in comprehensive schools seem to think that at about 750 something begins to crack. This is not to say that there are not excellent schools of 1000 or more, but they usually have exceptional staff, and will probably be divided into small communities. Cities have grown and grown, and the problems of the massive conurbations seem almost unanswerable. The ancient Greek *polis* or city-state was a community in which each citizen counted. Athens, by far the largest of them, had a population of about a quarter of a million. The latest thinking on the development of new towns in Britain and America, such as Milton Keynes or Trendon, suggests that they should not exceed a quarter of a million.

'Small is beautiful' can be an unduly limiting concept. But the theories and practice of unlimited expansion have proved disastrous. 'Small is beautiful' is a good catchphrase to call us back to an alternative society.

It was not for her size, power or riches that God chose Israel. Amos cried out about her smallness (Amos 7.2), but God still loved her. We shall go far wrong if we despise the day of small things (Zech. 4.10). The God who brings down the high tree and exalts the low tree (Ezek. 17.24) is the same God who chooses the things which are not, to bring to nothing the things which are (1 Cor. 1.28).

The Christian church has here something to contribute which could revitalise society. There has been argument about church government now across the centuries and millennia. We are increasingly coming to see that a sound structure will incorporate elements from the various traditions. It is not merely that some Christians hold to an episcopal hierarchy as of the essence of the church, and others with equal fervour to the local church meeting, so that if we are to draw together at all, we shall have to find a structure which includes both. It is that we need some kind of centralisation to act on a world scale (we may think of Christian Aid, or of the Missionary Societies, or of the consultative status of the World Council of Churches with the UN); we need local involvement to exist at all.

We have already glanced at Paul's vision of the church, many limbs or members in one body, each with its own particular function. I do not think that many Christians think in this way or that many local churches operate so as to encourage them to think in this way. Yet if churches did so operate, so that every member had a part in the strategy and tactics of their church's fight against evil and in the battle for a more loving world, and that every member played an appropriate part in determining that strategy, we might be learning something about 'grass-roots democracy'.

Christians in industry might do much more. The Scott Bader Commonwealth is avowedly an attempt to apply the Quaker Peace Testimony to business activity. It is based upon the belief that the ultimate criteria in the organisation of work should be human dignity and service, not economic considerations exclusively, 'an involvement in the society in which one shares, joining the inward purpose in solidarity and the outward purpose of identification, the motivating power going beyond rights and duties to embrace responsibility for society'. This has meant what Ernest Bader calls co-decision, which is not the same as Partnership in Management or Co-ownership in Industry. To have one of the two Union representatives on a board of management is a sop to Cerberus: it is mere tokenism. Co-decision does not mean that the management retain the power but graciously condescend to listen to workers. It means that decisive power rests with the members in General Meeting. It was a unanimous vote in General Meeting which established the Commonwealth in 1951. The members become involved in a nexus of interrelated rights and responsibilities – the right to participate in the processes of making decisions and fixing pay, and the right to an equitable share in the common product of work, together with the responsibility for good workmanship and for acquiring the interest, information and understanding needed if decisions are to be informed and effective – and the responsibility is not to 'them', but to one another, to 'us'. Plainly such a pattern is possible only in a relatively small concern. Here, certainly, small is beautiful. Scott Bader have a staff of 450, but only those aged eighteen and over, with 18 months' service, are voting members: 260 in all. The advantages of size are easy to exaggerate. The large organisation may sometimes be necessary; if so it must be broken up into units of such a size that the individual can both feel and be responsible.

It is not just the size of the Commonwealth. Scott Bader have found the necessity to operate through the work group of seven to twelve people 'so as to develop a sense of responsibility to make the work situation a truly human one and to allow people to develop the kind of knowledge and understanding which enables them to participate in decision-making'. Ernest Bader is insistent that, provided there exists the necessary goodwill for a united realistic purpose of service not greed, and that there is real common ownership not just nationalisation, and that the work-force is arranged in small decentralised semi-autonomous units, there is no reason why industrial democracy cannot be successfully practised even in the largest undertakings.

Universities are notoriously undemocratic institutions, even considering the members of staff alone as the citizen-body. To open the main decision-making body, say, the senate, to all members of staff can be self-defeating. Occasionally, on a major issue, public opinion is provoked to assert itself, and this is healthy, but in general the body becomes too unwieldy for effective discussion and the meetings fall into disrepute. Lecturers do their own thing in lecture-room, lab and library, and that is it. The Open University began without departments, and there remains no official departmental structure. The unit was and is the faculty, and we in the Arts Faculty from the first had a weekly meeting of all the faculty; this is now fortnightly, and I do not myself feel that the change is for the better. However, it still means that virtually every matter of public concern is discussed by the whole faculty, that every member of staff can properly feel that at this, the most significant level, they have a full say in what goes forward. Further, we seldom take votes, and would be unlikely to accept a decision by a narrow majority; if it were a matter of internal faculty business we would accept it only if the minority agreed to go forward on this basis; if it were a matter to be forwarded for university decision we would record the disagreement. This principle of operation extends to the preparation of courses. Professors and lecturers with us do not simply do their own thing. They operate as members of a team, an experience both traumatic and enriching, and one very largely new in university teaching. The syllabus, its division into component parts, the use of radio, television, and the written word, the number and nature of the assignments, the provision and structure of summer school or day school, the scope of individual responsibilities, are all determined by the course-team operating as a whole. Further, each individual block of work is assigned to something not unlike the Scott Bader work-group.

In all these ways we have achieved two things not commonly found in universities: each individual member of staff has a genuine responsibility for the communal decisions; each individual member of staff is continually working, not in isolation but as a member of a team.

Plainly with a student body scattered to the four winds we cannot associate students with the taking of decisions in the same way. It is a matter of some importance that there are student members of key University boards, simply so that the views of students are not forgotten. But the study-centres which are to be found in the main centres of population, nearly three hundred of them, are the places where students come into their own, not merely with the self-help academic groups (which operate in areas too small for a study-centre as well), but in giving each study-centre a social and intellectual life of its own.

The part which students properly play in the life of universities, and still more of schools, it not an easy one to determine. Universities, colleges and schools have an ongoing life far beyond the few years of any individual student's participation, and student majorities should not determine all policies. At the same time, university students are now adult, voting members of the political community, and it is impossible to treat them as there simply to obey rules which others have made. Furthermore, if an education system is designed to train people for life, and we desire to see developing something more like a participatory democracy, then it is important that there shall be elements of participatory democracy during the formative period, and these must involve genuine responsibility, and not the sort of token placing of an odd student on committees where they can do no harm, or the formation of schools councils which become talking-shops with no powers.

In voluntary organisations too there is room for decentralisation. A group from the Fellowship of Reconciliation, forming a 'collective' in Manchester have recently written:

The negative effect of a hierarchical and centralised office is considerable; it creates a centre to which the membership looks to *take* initiatives as well as to carry them out and support local projects; the dependence of local groups on the central office tends to lead to inertia and inaction. It puts a huge burden of responsibility on to the General Secretary and the other 'officers', and traps the other office staff in the more boring, routine and repetitive jobs – typing, duplicating, mailing, filing, etc. The strain placed on the few is too great: other office staff are denied the possibility, should they wish it, of developing their potential for more satisfying and creative work; and the scattered membership find it increasingly difficult to work as part of a dynamic local structure with a life of its own. (*Reconciliation Quarterly* Dec. 1975, p. 19)

Historically this ignores the fact that it is very largely the decay in once powerful local groups which has led to the strains at the centre. Practically it underestimates the need for a strong central organisation for national witness, for co-ordination, for making available literature and other means of communication, and for opening up new action in areas where there is no local initiative. But it is entirely right in its warnings, and in its stress on dynamic local structures.

When we come to the residential and political community, Britain is largely structured towards elections not towards participation. Yet the finest example of participatory democracy which I have experienced was in a parish meeting in our own little village. The old school was packed out, the council representatives were not allowed to get away with doubtful decisions, there was very wide participation in debate, and the voting was clear and enthusiastic. The private comment of one villager was more than an immediate witticism: 'If we had this every night, there'd be no need of TV.'

It was exciting to find a Christian radical student writing in *Movement* of his rediscovery of G. K. Chesterton. He found that Chesterton stood for many of the things which he himself yearned for. He found in Distributism a twentieth-century version of the Year of Jubilee. He found in the fantasy of *The Napoleon of Notting Hill* the philosophy of decentralisation, the poetry of limitations, patriotism without imperialism. Chesterton was deeply estranged from the Boer War; he hated it for its cheerfulness and its vile assurance of victory. He found himself identified with the small farming commonwealth which was threatened by a cosmopolitan empire.

Chesterton was at the time something of a socialist, 'because the only alternative to being a socialist was not being a socialist'. He went along with Shaw and Wells, because he loathed the plutocracy. He would today be adamant in opposition to all multi-national corporations. Then, wandering round Notting Hill he had a vision. His Progressive friends were as keen as the plutocrats on destroying Notting Hill. When they said 'Every day in every way better and better' they meant 'bigger and bigger'. 'In that half-second of time, gazing with rapt admiration at the row of little shops, nobly flanked by a small pub and a small church, I discovered that not only was I against the plutocrats, I was against the idealists. In the comparatively crystalline air of that romantic village I heard the clear call of a trumpet. And, once for all, I drew my sword – purchased in the old curiosity shop – in defence of Notting Hill.'

In the book the eccentric king Auberon Quin proclaims the Charter of the Free Cities. Hammersmith and Kensington, Bayswater and Chelsea, Battersea, Clapham and Balham, are restored to their ancient magnificence. For most it is a tedious charade. But in Notting Hill the Provost is a redheaded romantic named Adam Wayne, who will not let a little road named Pump Street be torn up to be exploited by big business, and asserts the independence of Notting Hill. And it is when in response to his cries of 'Notting Hill!' that he hears one of his opponents raise the cry of 'Bayswater!' that he senses himself victorious.

The Napoleon of Notting Hill is not about participatory democracy. It is a vision not a programme, a fantasy far removed from fact. But a healthy society depends vitally upon such local pride, local loyalty, local participation and local responsibility, and the more that responsible decisions can be decentralised to the points where people can participate and can feel that they belong, the healthier. Such a concept is totally different from that of the plebiscite. This may have occasional merit as a means of elucidating the majority view on a larger issue, but those voting remain remote from the level at which decisions are really being taken.

A word of warning must be voiced. Those who believe intensely in decentralisation often also believe intensely that they know what is right for society at large. Decentralisation is incompatible, except within broad limits, with the imposition of strong central policies. The more widely shared decision-making becomes, the less likely the result is to be just what we want. The Lord in his infinite mercy has made us very various. This is a blessing, if we will receive it as such. Decentralisation means variety. It means flexibility. It is not administratively tidy. It is open, and openness means unpredictability.

7

No more Jew and Greek: The open society

There is neither Jew nor Greek, there is neither slave nor
free, there is neither male nor female; for you are all one in
Christ Jesus.

Galatians 3.28

In his great work *The Two Sources of Religion and Morality* Henri
Bergson draws a vital distinction between the Closed Society and
the Open Society. The Closed Society is one of many, each
marked off from the other, and mutually exclusive. The bond of
cohesion is danger from other closed societies. War, hot or cold,
provides a good example of such cohesion. A few years ago a man
was executed for murder. A newspaper reporter in search of a
story visited his widow, and commented on a medal on the
mantelpiece. 'That,' she said, 'they gave him that the last time he
killed a man.' What is virtue when done to those outside the
closed society is treason when done to those within.

The Open Society is inclusive: it has no frontier: it embraces
all mankind: it does not know the word 'enemy': its cohesion
comes not from fear but from love. It too has its own morality, a
single moral law which can be analysed into the two propo-
sitions: 'All men are brothers' and 'I am my brother's keeper.'

There is no process of natural growth from the closed to the
open society. 'Never' wrote Bergson 'shall we pass from the
closed society to the open society, from the city to humanity, by
any mere broadening out. The two things are not of the same
essence.' You can build higher forms of the closed society, but
they are still based on fear. The USA and USSR are no nearer the

open society than were their constituent states, and the American and Russian blocks are no nearer the open society than the USA and USSR; nor will closer economic and political ties transform Western Europe into an open society. It is the saints, mystics and heroes who will bring the world community. So Bergson, and though we may think his dichotomy between the spiritual and the political too rigid, he is fundamentally right.

The moralities of these two societies differ totally, as rest differs from movement. The morality of the closed society is legalistic, easy to pinpoint, inflexible. The morality of the open society is personal, open, hard to catch within the pincers of a rule.

The distinction is basic. In 1968-9 I was serving as Visiting Professor at Hampton Institute in Virginia, one of the oldest and greatest of the predominantly Black universities. There we met the Rev. Metz Rollins, Director of the League of Black Churchmen, and a member (like ourselves) of the Fellowship of Reconciliation. We asked him how he could, at one and the same time, be Director of an organisation which was, on the face of it, divisive, and a member of a body which stood for reconciliation. He answered: 'Integration, even in the liberal north, has meant that individual Blacks are welcomed into white society, provided that they conform and stick to the established rules and established pattern of culture. This is not what we want. We want the Open Society, in which different individuals and groups can enter, bringing their distinctive contributions, *which change the whole*. And if the Black people are going to do this, we must find our own identity, and for this we must stand apart. Of course it is dangerously divisive, but it is a risk which must be taken.'

As we look across the pages of history Christianity has too often been associated with the attitudes of the closed society. But is this of the essence of Christianity?

The view that ultimate reality is static and unchanging comes not from Jesus but from Plato – and, as is too often forgotten, Plato himself came to reject it.

STRANGER: Good God, are we going to be so easily persuaded

that movement, life, soul, intelligence really and truly have no place in ultimate reality, that ultimate reality lacks life and intelligence, but exists in mindless majesty and static immobility?

THEAETETUS: That would be a terrible position to take, sir.

STRANGER: Then are we to say that it possesses intelligence but not life?

THEAETETUS: Impossible!

STRANGER: Are we then saying that it incorporates both these, but not in a soul?

THEAETETUS: But in what other way could it do so?

STRANGER: Are we then saying that it is endowed with intelligence, life and soul, but despite its soul, is utterly immobile and static?

THEAETETUS: I find the whole idea quite absurd!

STRANGER: So we must admit that motion and movement are a part of existence?

THEAETETUS: Yes.

STRANGER: Our conclusion is that if there were absolute immobility there would be no intelligence anywhere in the universe.

(Plato, *Sophist*, 248E–9B)

(Our word 'soul' has acquired overtones from which the Greek *psyche* is free, but it is hard to find an alternative.) Plato thus came to the view that there is a dynamic element in ultimate reality.

For the Christian ultimate reality lies in God, the God who made man and woman in his own image and who is not less than personal, the God whose natural appellation is 'Father', the God who is active in Creation, and perhaps (according to one modern cosmology) in 'continuous creation', the God who sustains his world and makes the corn and vines grow, the God whose being is love (which is not a Platonic abstract but a personal activity), the God who is Lord of history and led the Israelites out of Egypt, the God of Abraham, Isaac and Jacob, the living God of the living, the God who makes *all* things new. For the Christian ultimate reality is personal, dynamic, unexpected and unpredictable. How can this living, dynamic God call us to a closed or static society?

For the Christian God is revealed in a human life in Jesus Christ. He who has seen Jesus has seen the Father. In Jesus the Word, the Reason and Pattern of the Universe, the *Tao*, takes flesh. But Jesus himself grew and changed. He was open to all sorts and conditions of humanity, and responded to each. He did not turn away from the company of his closest disciples his betrayer or his denier. He shared with them his vision of the life in God, but he imposed it on none of them. The temptations in the wilderness were temptations to compel submission by bribery, magic or political and military power. He did not succumb. It was open to his people to reject his way of love; he foresaw that the consequences would be violent uprising and even more violent suppression, and wept over the suffering that would come; but he did not compel them. He did not come to be a lawgiver.

And God is revealed in his Spirit. Paul in his cosmic vision in Romans 8 sees the sufferings of the present time as the birthpangs of a new age. No closed society there, but the readiness for the unexpected! And as we pray for a new and changed humanity, the very Spirit of God is alongside us in our prayers. For this is the Creator Spirit who moved on the face of the waters to bring the universe out of primal chaos, and who moves among us now to inspire a new world. But not lightly. Not predictably. Not in such a way as to be captured within a closed society. William Temple put it powerfully: in *Readings in St. John's Gospel*.

When we pray 'Come Holy Ghost, our souls inspire', we had better know what we are about. He will not carry us to easy triumphs and gratifying successes; more probably He will set us to some task for God in the full intention that we shall fail, so that others, learning wisdom by our failure, may carry the good cause forward! He may take us through loneliness, desertion by friends, apparent desertion even by God; that was the way Christ went to the Father. He may drive us into the wilderness to be tempted of the devil. He may lead us from the Mount of Transfiguration (if He ever lets us climb it) to the hill that is called the Place of a Skull. For if we invoke Him, it must be to help us in doing God's will, not ours. We cannot call upon the

> Creator Spirit, by whose aid
> The world's foundations first were laid

in order to use omnipotence for the supply of our futile pleasures or the success of our futile plans. If we invoke Him we must be ready for the glorious pain of being caught by His power out of our petty orbit into the eternal purposes of the Almighty, in whose onward sweep our lives are as a speck of dust. The soul that is filled with the Spirit must have become purged of all pride or love of ease, all self-complacence and self-reliance; but that soul has found the only real dignity, the only lasting joy. Come then, Great Spirit, come. Convict the world and convict my timid soul.

The living Spirit of the living God blows where he wills.

The being of God is love; the way of life revealed by Jesus is love; the first fruit of the Spirit is love. The morality of the open society stands to the morality of the closed society precisely as love to law, as the Sermon on the Mount to the *Torah*. Conversely, for those who have embraced Christ's way of love, who have received his love and seek that his love may overflow from them to others, there is no such thing as a closed society.

> He drew a circle that shut me out—
> Heretic, rebel, a thing to flout.
> But Love and I had the wit to win:
> We drew a circle that took him in.
> Edwin Markham, *Outwitted*

God loves us as we are. He sends his sun to shine and his rain to fall upon just and unjust alike. He shows his love for us in that while we were yet sinners Christ died for us. If God so loved us, ought we not much more to love one another? John (1.12) says that Jesus gives us the right to become children of God. The Church is never the Church unless it is going into all lands and to all peoples with the good news of the fellowship of all men with one another, with Christ and with God, a fellowship which they have only to enter, only to receive. It is the Christian mission that all men find their true selves in becoming children of God and brothers of one another, that Parthians, Medes, Elamites, inhabitants of Mesopotamia, of Judea and Cappadocia, of Pontus and Asia, of Phrygia and Pamphylia, of Egypt, and all the rest, enter the Pentecostal community (Acts 2.9–11). And while they become one in Christ Jesus, they retain their differences of tradition and experience, as different limbs of a single body.

All human endeavours are imperfect. All are besmirched by sin. Never can we say that we have nothing more to learn. We may put alongside one another Cromwell's words to the General Assembly of the Church of Scotland, 'I beseech you, in the bowels of Christ, think it possible you may be mistaken', and those of the Pilgrim Father John Robinson, 'The Lord hath yet more light and truth to break forth from his Holy Word.' The Christian is sure of some things, but he must not be like Macaulay, of whom Melbourne said, 'I wish I were as cocksure of anything as Tom Macaulay is of everything.' Our very righteousness is a torn and dirty dress.

So that we are drawn to the open society alike by humility about ourselves, and by our love and respect for others. There is no man through whom God may not speak. He who in the old story spoke through the voice of an ass may surely speak through Nick Bottom. Goldsmith's vicar of Wakefield showed a wise humanity in always conversing with strangers, for they would learn from him, or he from them. We do not know where we may encounter the Christ. Turgeniev has an exquisite little parable.

I saw myself, in dream, a youth, almost a boy, in a low-low-pitched wooden church. The slim wax candles gleamed, spots of red, before the old pictures of the saints.

A ring of coloured light encircled each tiny flame. Dark and dim it was in the church. But there stood before me many people. All fair-headed, peasant heads. From time to time they began swaying, falling, rising again, like the ripe ears of wheat, when the wind of summer passes in slow undulation over them.

All at once some man came up from behind and stood beside me.

I did not turn towards him; but at once I felt that this man was Christ.

Emotion, curiosity, awe overmastered me suddenly. I made an effort . . . and looked at my neighbour.

A face like every one's, a face like all men's faces. The eyes looked a little upwards, quietly and intently. The lips closed, but not compressed; the upper lip, as it were, resting on the lower; a small beard parted in two. The hands folded and still. And the clothes on him like every one's.

'What sort of Christ is this?' I thought. 'Such an ordinary, ordinary man! It can't be!'

I turned away. But I had hardly turned my eyes away from this ordinary man when I felt again that it really was none other than Christ standing beside me.

Again I made an effort over myself . . . And again the same face, like all men's faces, the same everyday though unknown features.

And suddenly my heart sank, and I came to myself. Only then I realised that just such a face – a face like all men's faces – is the face of Christ.

The Christ who says that the cup of water given to the thirsty is given to him may be encountered in any thirsty person, whatever their creed, colour and culture.

None of us dares say we have a Christian society, within the Church or outside; indeed one man, who served half his days as a Member of Parliament and half as a minister of the Church of Scotland, declared that he had been involved in quite as many compromises, and quite as much corrupt dealing in the latter rôle as in the former. The most we could say is that some societies, in T. S. Eliot's term, have been Christianised. They have been exposed to Christianity; but that does not make them Christian. It does not make them closer to the mind of Christ than societies which have never encountered Christianity.

In his masterly exposition *Christ and Culture* H. Richard Niebuhr identifies five attitudes which Christians have taken to secular culture. The first emphasises the *opposition* between Christ and culture. Whatever the social customs and human achievements of the surrounding culture, Christ is opposed to them; men must choose; there is an 'either-or'. This is illustrated by Tertullian and Tolstoy. The second recognises a fundamental *agreement* between Christ and culture. Western Christians assume this uncritically, but so in Eastern Europe sometimes do Christian Marxists. Historical examples include Abelard and Ritschl. In the third view Christ is the fulfilment of cultural aspirations but above and beyond them. Niebuhr calls this a *synthetic* view and exemplifies it by Thomas Aquinas. The fourth attitude acknowledges a dualism of Christ and culture, each with proper and authoritative claims, which are held in *polarity and tension*. This is the characteristic Lutheran view. In the fifth view the opposition and tension is recognised, but it may become transmuted. For Christ converts man, according to this view, not out of his culture but in his culture. This *conversionist* solution is propounded by Augustine and worked out by Calvin.

Thus we cannot work within a certainty that we have nothing to learn from other cultures. In three of these views Christ stands in opposition to and tension with our culture, whatever it is; in one he challenges it from beyond. Only in the second is there agreement between Christ and culture – but this is found in different cultures. Christ transcends them all, and we may learn about him through his agreement with other cultures than our own.

Even if our culture were more strongly Christianised our loyalty to Christ would still call us to openness. Even if it were more strongly unified we should have hesitations about seeing our human relativities as divine absolutes. But in fact our culture

87

is an amalgam of influences from Athens, Rome and Jerusalem, shaped, moulded and changed by the forces of history, through the widening of the frontiers of the mind and of the known world at the Renaissance, through the Industrial Revolution and the Automotive Revolution. It has within itself many facets and many subcultures. Within the world, western technological culture is one among many, and some of those others incorporate values easier to reconcile with the New Testament than individualistic capitalism. Christians are a small minority in the world. They are a small minority in nominally Christian Britain. Our society is, in the jargon, pluralist, and that fact is, potentially, a vast enrichment.

Paul in his comprehensive vision of the work of Christ declares that in Christ there is no such thing as Jew and Greek, slave and freeman, male and female; all are one person in Christ Jesus (Gal. 3.28). In putting on Christ we discard, not our background and culture, for we cannot do that, but the ultimately divisive aspects of them (Gal. 3.8–14), the strident, self-assertive proclamation of cultural, national and racial superiority which invariably springs from the uncertainties of an inferiority complex.

In the society which the Christian seeks, racial and national differences become irrelevant. It is appalling that we in Britain are still speaking of 'immigrants'; nearly half our coloured population are born in Britain. It is appalling to hear Christians speak of 'tolerating' other human beings – *tolerating* men and women made in God's image, *tolerating* those for whom Christ died. The Black American comedian Dick Gregory once broke into his patter before a white audience to comment 'Say, folk, wouldn't it be something if this was only burnt cork, and you was all being tolerant for nothing?'

There is much ignorance. A hostel warden in Bedford, John Brown, welcoming immigrant (genuinely!) workers from Europe, the Caribbean, and the Indian sub-continent, drew some important conclusions.

1. The European immigrants face the same problems as the rest.
2. Problems arise not from colour but from culture.

3. None of the immigrant groups wants to be totally assimilated: they want to maintain their distinctive identity.

4. In Bedford the crime-rate among immigrants is lower than among the native Britons.

5. Strained relations with the police, which do exist, are due not to the prevalence of crime but to difficulties in communication.

6. All the immigrant groups dislike the permissiveness of British society.

7. It is the young immigrants who become absorbed in the host community who get into most trouble.

There is plenty there to make us think.

In July 1975 *The Milton Keynes Express* carried a supplement dealing with the cosmopolitan character of the new city. 'Some of the people have travelled thousands of miles to make a new life, others have lived here for years. All have a common link – they are citizens of Milton Keynes.' The supplement richly and warmly illustrated with colour photographs, emphasised integration: one photo labelled 'Haggis and Saris' showed six Indian ladies celebrating Burns night. But not integration at the expense of cultural roots but through mutual enrichment. 'Racial integration must not mean the modelling of everyone on John Bull and swamping of non-British culture' and an organization named ROOTS exists to foster such enrichment. So when people congregate in their own racial or national or cultural groups we should understand it (for the British do exactly the same abroad) and welcome it, and find means for group encounter. The issue, which contained news stories of Pakistanis and Poles, Scots and Welsh and Irish, Italians and Austrians, Indians and Chinese, was responsible journalism of the best kind, and more of it would lead to a healthier and happier community everywhere.

If, with George Fox, we believe in 'that of God in every man', we believe in the Open Society. The more aware we are of our own sinfulness, individual and corporate, the more aware we are that a closed society cannot reveal the way of God. The more we look to the living God, to the openness of Jesus to all men, to the glorious uncontrollable unpredictability of the Spirit, the less we can have to do with closed societies. The secret is love. If we really love our neighbour, the Sikh, the Pakistani, the Jamaican in our midst, we shall seek to lead him to Christ, but we shall love him as he is with all his experiences and traditions so richly different from ours, and we could not try to force him into conformity with our own, though we may hope that he will learn from ours, as we from his, and in the dialectic of history we shall move on to a fuller synthesis. The Open Society has love as its ethic. Love leads us into the Open Society.

In the society which the Christian seeks, class differences are irrelevant. Christ breaks down the barriers of class. Those barriers are still strong in British society. A small statistic. In 1961, 68.9 per cent of final year medical students in Britain were drawn from the two highest social classes, 31.1 per cent from the three lowest. By 1966 these figures had changed to 75.7 per cent and 24.2 per cent respectively. The proportion of the population in the first group is 18.3 per cent, in the second 81.7 per cent. All animals are equal, but some are very definitely more equal than others. The impressions of visitors from overseas and sociological investigation alike show that Britain is class-ridden, perhaps the most class-ridden nation in the world. In November 1975 the Archbishop of Canterbury made a very moderate proposal that those with an income of £6,000 a year or over should make a modest contribution to the needs of those in what are called the 'lower-income brackets'. *The Daily Telegraph* carried some letters on the subject. One correspondent said that he had no intention of paying to have nice semi-detached houses replaced by a concrete jungle of high-rise flats. It has now been amply shown that the predilection of town-planners for high-rise flats was an error, though an honest one, and it is unlikely that new building will continue along those lines. But the people who exist with one or more families in a single dark rat-infested room would be profoundly grateful even for the concrete jungle: so would the letter-writer if he were in their position. He obviously has no idea of what is going on around him. Another writer said he had no intention of giving up anything as long as an unemployed

Irish labourer with eleven children was receiving £67 a week at public expense. The fact that the man is Irish seems hardly relevant; the fact that he is prepared to labour might be a point of contrast with the writer of the letter. £67 divided by 13 is roughly £5. £5 a week per person is £250 a year. It would be interesting to see how the writer would manage on that.

The barriers remain in the Church. It was admittedly (thank God!) an unusual church, but I knew a down-town church in an industrial city in which, in the years after the second World War, a church family party to welcome a new minister was held in full evening dress. They had a Ladies' Meeting on Monday and a Women's Meeting on Tuesday – yes, really and truly. They treated the caretaker like a doormat, wiping their feet on him. After a social gathering he was left with all the clearing up to do; when one or two of us suggested that we might lend a hand we were told that he was paid to do it. When the daughter of a skilled carpenter from the industrial area started coming to the church, the members were incredulous – 'Does your father actually work in industry?' – and the mothers cold-shouldered her because they thought she had come to steal their precious sons. Yet these were nice people, and they had a sincere allegiance to Christ, but they had not allowed him to take over their lives and break down the barriers in their hearts and minds.

Something of this attitude continues to pervade the churches. Not long ago the secretary of a church in an expanding town came to a church meeting with good news: 'They are building a new estate near us – not council houses, but detached and semi-detached – *they'll be our sort of people*.' But whatever houses they lived in they would be God's sort of people. For the most part – the Roman Catholics and Salvation Army have been obvious exceptions – the life and liturgy of the churches in England have been cogged in to middle-class modes of thinking and living, and recent experiments have done little to alter this. It is a humbling and profitable exercise to remember that if anyone felt unfamiliar on first entry into the early church it was those from the middle and upper classes. There were not many men of wisdom by human standards there, not many powerful or highly born (1 Cor. 1.26). Late in the second century Celsus in attacking the Christians draws the same picture; their teachers are wool-dressers, cobblers, fullers, the most vulgar and uneducated persons. One sometimes wonders whether Simon Peter would have found a home in the Church of Christ today, let alone been accepted for the ministry; the mind dances at what he would have made of a theological college.

We Christians must break down the barriers in our own churches; for if there are barriers there we have not given ourselves fully to Christ. And we seek a society in which each is accepted for what he is. A naive parallel is the cricket or football team. There are no barriers there; a common purpose, respect for each person for what he is, both as a games-player and a man, teamwork, and friendship break them down. Indeed G. M. Trevelyan once suggested that Britain was saved from the French Revolution because the aristocrats played cricket with the commoners; perhaps the parallel is not so naive. We seek the extension of this spirit to society as a whole, and the erosion of privilege. To stick a label on a person, capitalist or communist, whitey or nigger, middle-class or working-class, is to fail to see him as a person. The girl who cried out in a heated interracial meeting 'I'm not whitey, I'm me!' was breaking through the barrier of the label. To treat a person as a person is a step towards loving them. Love leads to the Open Society.

In the society which the Christian seeks the difference between men and women is also irrelevant. Of course this does not mean that we all become hermaphrodites. Men will not bear or breast-feed the children, though they might well play and are increasingly playing a larger part in looking after them. There are physical differences. On the whole, men are physically stronger, though by no means tougher. There are also mental and intellectual and perhaps spiritual differences, though these are much harder to pinpoint. (It is a curious fact that, though any list of the world's great poets will include Sappho, and any similar list of novelists will contain Jane Austen, the Brontës and 'George Eliot', and any list of performing artists will have on it Siddons and Suggia and Schwartzkopf and Karsavina, it is unlikely that any women will appear in the 'first hundred' composers or painters, although these occupations have been fully open to them.)

But these characteristic differences belong to the masculine and feminine, not to particular men and women. It is easy to find some women who are more masculine than some men, some men who are more feminine than some women. So even if it be accepted that masculinity and femininity point to a difference of social function – and there are those who say that it is all a matter of social conditioning, not of inherent, innate distinction – still we should seek an open society with equality of opportunity.

It is in fact increasingly being seen and said that women are the most underused of our natural resources. New Zealand was the first nation to grant women the vote, as long ago as 1893. In 1972, 92 per cent of the candidates for Parliament in New Zealand and 95 per cent of those elected were men. (The highest percentages of women members of national legislatures are 35 per cent in the USSR and 21.5 per cent in Finland.) In the 1973 UN General Assembly there were 180 women to 2,369 men. 55 countries had no women on their delegation, 44 only one. It might be added that according to biologists the only animals in which the female is more aggressive than the male are the hamster and possibly the gibbon; a higher proportion of women in positions of political responsibility might well reduce international tensions, provided that they have not achieved their position by outdoing the men in an aggressively masculine world. G. A. Studdert-Kennedy, 'Woodbine Willie', speaking to women in 1928 said, 'I wonder do you realise how much depends on you? There is the battle of two standards, which is it going to be? You have broken out of the home and taken up your work again. You have come back to the centre of things. But O, for Christ's sake remember that you must carry a home in your heart. You must make the world a home. You must inspire the warrior man to build it. You must make him turn from war to work. You must say to him, "I will not bear babies to be made cannon fodder of." You must not go back into the home and shut the doors. There are a thousand problems that you must help to solve.' Nearly fifty years later that message is still needed.

It is salutary to remember that the first countries with women Prime Ministers in recent times were all in Asia, Sri Lanka, India and Israel. Mme Elizabeth Domitien, in the Central African Republic, recently became Africa's first woman Prime Minister. Sierra Leone provides the only woman director of a World Bank project in the world. There the professional head of the Ministry of Health is a woman; so is the Registrar of the Supreme Court, and the professional head of the Ministry of Social Welfare. Sierra Leoneans, in referring to the place of women in society, speak of Darkest Britain and Darkest America. The world has far to go on the road of sexual equality. International Women's Year in 1975 was a step, but only a small step along the road.

The churches have far to go. Even our image of God needs changing. For the great word of Genesis 1.27, 'So God created man in his own image; in the image of God created he him; male and female created he them' means that the image of God is male-and-female. And, of course, this must be. All power comes from God and is of God; all that is good and lovely comes from God and is of God. There is a familiar story of a Russian astronaut coming from outer space and being asked, 'Did you see God? Ha! Ha!' 'As a matter of fact I did.' 'What! But you can't have! He doesn't exist. What was he like? Was he as we've always imagined him?' 'As a matter of fact, she's black.' That story ought not to startle us. But it does.

It is not easy to see that the physiological differences between men and women are relevant to the exercise of the ministry of the Word and Sacraments. There is change here. In Britain the Methodist Church has accepted women into the ministry. The Episcopal Church of Canada has voted in favour of the ordination of women. So has the Episcopal Church of the United States. Even at Rome they can joke about it: it is said that at the next Vatican Council the bishops will bring their wives; at the one following, they will bring their husbands. But, accepted in the

94

ministry, the women ministers must be given full responsibility and fair opportunity; this has not always happened in the past. There is great need for more women in the responsible councils of the churches. The British Council of Churches is deeply concerned about this but can do little until the constituent churches do more to place women in positions of responsibility. Too much of the church is clergy-ridden; they do not realise that there are laity, let alone women, in the churches.

A society in which men and women share in equal partnership and with mutual respect is likely to be a sexually healthier society. There is less danger of women – or men, for matter of that – being mere sex-objects. There is less danger of women, no longer confined to being secretaries, nurses and teachers, shop assistants, canteen servers and factory workers, but having genuine opportunities of fulfilment in widely different areas, simply turning their sexual powers to commercial ends. *Eros* has its natural place in human relations. But *eros* needs to be controlled by *agape*, love in the New Testament sense. It is this love which is the ethic of the Open Society, and love, Christian love, directs us into the Open Society.

8
Put up your sword: Nonviolence

And behold, one of those who were with Jesus stretched out his hand and drew his sword, and struck the slave of the high priest, and cut off his ear. Then Jesus said to him, 'Put your sword back into its place; for all who take the sword will perish by the sword.'

Matthew 26.51–2

Two clear facts confront us about the modern world. First, we could relatively easily solve the economic problems of a needy world if we would divert our energies and resources from weapons of war, which at best will never be used, and at worst will lead to the annihilation of mankind. World expenditure on arms is approaching $300,000,000,000 a year. $3 will save 100 children from blindness caused by vitamin deficiency. One Lightning aircraft costs as much as 570 kidney machines; one Phantom aircraft as much as 700 council houses; one submarine as much as one and a half hospitals; one through-deck cruiser as much as two new towns. The sum we spend on arms is already equal to the total amount spent by the whole world on basic foodstuffs, cereals, dairy products, fruit and vegetables and meat. It is growing so rapidly that at the present rate of expansion by the end of the century it will equal the total present wealth of the world. This is fantastic, nightmarish. DISARM OR PERISH is written on the wall of the world. We are failing to feed the hungry and to care for the sick, and the judgement which Jesus pronounces in the parable of the sheep and the goats is unequivocal. To say 'Ah! but we needed the money for armaments,' will be no defence upon the Day of Wrath. And the judgement, be it remembered, is upon the nations.

Even in the coldest, most calculating, prudential terms our practice does not make sense. At the height of the Vietnam War that witty American columnist Mort Malkin propounded a Grand Plan to bring it to an end. In sum: $20,000 to *every* member of the NLF to enable him to set up in business; private villas on the Riviera for all South Vietnam generals; a year's salary to an international commission of 100,000 men to organise peaceable elections, complete with computers to support them; $5,000,000,000 to replant South Vietnam; $3,000,000,000 to build up the North Vietnam economy to peaceable prosperity; and, for good measure, $5 a head to pacify every individual in the US, 'hawks, doves, parrots and chickens'. *The total cost once for all, would have equalled the average cost of a single year of the war.* It would be ludicrous, were it not so deeply tragic. We take a false step in good faith, and we have not the courage to admit our error. We become caught up in the logic of our folly.

There are those who say that nuclear weapons have made war unthinkable. It is hard for anyone with a sense of history to adopt so facile a view. Alfred Nobel's dream that his invention of cordite as a basis for explosives would put an end to wars by making them too dangerous proved to be a tragic mistake. We shall make the same mistake if we rely on fear of the hydrogen bomb.

For the piling-up of armaments itself springs from nothing but fear. It is the very antithesis of the way of Christ. There is no fear in love; if we fear, we do not, in a full sense, love. 'Never take a decision through fear,' said Fridtjof Nansen. 'You are never so likely to be wrong.'

The second clear fact of our time is that there are millions of people living under oppressive régimes of one sort or another. Sometimes they are openly authoritarian, sometimes the mailed fist is gloved in velvet. Sometimes they are openly racist, sometimes they profess 'tolerance' and practise paternalism from a standpoint of superiority. Sometimes they claim to be democratic but power rests with the rich. The Roman Catholic archbishop, Helder Camara, has affirmed that the primary violence is structural violence, social violence, the violence which is done to those who have small opportunities to attain that fullness of life which others enjoy unquestioningly. The people at the top may not be evil men in any obvious sense; in any obvious sense they may be good men, but blind. The violence is in the system. But those who rest in privilege, comfortably indifferent to what is happening to others, are not guiltless. Within Britain everyone who is likely to be reading this book is guilty, with the author, of structural violence. Within the community of the world everyone in Britain is so guilty.

It is an ineluctable law that violence tends to breed violence. The great American sociologist Pitimir Sorokin declared that social philosophy could be summed up in six words, 'Hate breeds hate. Love breeds love.' So Helder Camara calls us to break through the spiral of violence and replace it with a spiral of love.

But it needs a breakthrough. Those who are oppressed seek a violent solution, not because they are violent people, but because they are provoked by violence and because they can see no other way. Yet the very violence to which they are driven will divert their course from its intended end. In his brilliantly original book *Liberation Ethics*, John M. Swomley, Jr., argues that the goal of history is the liberation or redemption of man. Liberation ethics is concerned with freeing men and women from the structures of violence. These include institutional violence, racial discrimination, an economy which permits and maintains poverty, slavery, monopoly capitalism, war. Systems, not individuals, are the root of oppression. One of Marx's many insights was that the destruction of persons is not a key factor in transforming systems. The elimination or transformation of oppressive systems involves conflict leading to fundamental social change or revolution. A revolution need not be swift or violent. On the contrary violence destroys the revolution which it aims to produce. Liberation ethics is concerned with means as well as with ends, precisely because the means determine the ends. Violence is the same whether used by revolutionaries or by counter-revolutionaries. As Jacques Ellul puts it, 'Once you start using violence, you cannot get away from it.' That wise anarchist, Barthélemy de Ligt, once said 'The more violence, the less revolution.' Revolutions grow out of the disintegration of consent, not out of violence.

The great strength of *Liberation Ethics* lies in the careful sustenance of this position through case-studies. Swomley shows that violent revolution leads to a power-struggle among the revolutionary leaders, centralisation of power in the army, bureaucracy or both, external hostility, serious damage to the economy, continuing oppression. This is sustained by an examination of the Revolutions in Russia, China, Algeria, Cuba, the careers of Che Guevara and Camilo Torres, the attempt to assassinate Hitler. This last should be compulsory reading for all who idealise Bonhoeffer's heroic but naive involvement.

A classic instance of violence negating itself was seen in Nigeria in 1966. A state of tyranny had grown up in the Western Region, fostered by the Federal Government. The Yorubas, patient, slow to move, placed everything on the elections in October 1965. At those polls the popular vote ousted Chief Akintola's dictatorial régime, but those in power simply reversed the election figures and perpetuated their own autocracy. At this point the region exploded into bitter violence. There were rumours that the armies of the north were going to march down, and fears of an even more disastrous eruption. At this point a group of army majors of the Ibo tribe, in a brilliantly planned and co-ordinated operation, assassinated the main crooks and the honourable but weak Federal Prime Minister, who had in his hands the evidence of the rigged election, and took no action about it. The loss of life was relatively small, the sense of relief enormous. Yet those who saw further knew that violence breeds violence, and that the only lesson political assassination teaches is that political assassination is possible. The assassinations of January, which challenged the power of the northerners, were followed by the

July mutiny, which reasserted it. With that went a massacre of Ibos in the north; this was followed by a massacre of Hausas in Port Harcourt by Ibos (an episode carefully ignored by Biafran propaganda); and this by a still more abominable massacre of Ibos till the whole thing fell apart in a disastrous civil war.

Swomley gives five reasons for rejecting violence as a revolutionary method: the fact that the established order has control of violence; that violent revolution wipes out the good with the bad; that violent revolution cannot be controlled; that the revolutionary purpose is negated by violence; and that revolution directed against oppressive violence can succeed only if it can provide a nonviolent alternative structure.

Does Chirst offer an alternative way to violence?

Patently, the way of violence was not his. As we have seen He did not go along with those who wanted to overthrow Rome and establish the Kingdom of God by violence, the Zealots as they were later called. This, no doubt, was the Temptation to receive the kingdoms of the world on the devil's terms, and the vigour with which Jesus rejects Peter's protests against the concept of a suffering Messiah is precisely because he is renewing this temptation ('Away with you, Satan!'). He did not enter Jerusalem sword in hand upon a white horse, to bring war, but lowly upon an ass to bring peace (Zech. 9.9–10). But equally he did not go along with the Quislings and collaborators, or with those who treated the political scene as irrelevant. On the contrary, he was crucified, and knew that he was going to be crucified. Crucifixion was not the Jewish penalty for blasphemy; it was the Roman penalty for revolutionary subversion. Jesus was executed as a revolutionary, a nonviolent revolutionary. And he laid the same road upon his followers.

His teaching is explicit. One of the earliest records of the received Christian ethics is in Paul's letter to the Church in Rome (Rom. 12–13), which is explicit against 'resistance' to Rome. The way to counter evil is never with its own weapons. The enemy is to be greeted with active love. He may not respond, but our Christian way is to live peaceably with all, so far as it depends on us. We are not to be overcome by evil but to overcome evil with good. This is precisely what we find in Matthew in the Sermon on the Mount. Active love is the way to meet oppression; the injunction to go the second mile is related to the Roman soldier's right to conscribe a civilian to carry his pack for a mile. His response is irrelevant. Our love, nonviolent love, is to be as all-embracing as the weather, which is no respecter of persons, as all-embracing as God's love. Jesus' injunction of nonviolence is seen equally unequivocally in Gethsemane. There one of his followers, perhaps out of misdirected loyalty, seeks to defend him with the sword. Jesus's words, 'Put your sword back into its place: for all who take the sword will perish by the sword', were not addressed to an aggressor, but, as we might say, to a practitioner of defensive warfare. Tertullian says that in these words Jesus disarmed every soldier.

For two and a half centuries the central traditions of the Church stood for nonviolence. The Sermon on the Mount itself is not only the teaching of Jesus; it is also a record of the beliefs of the Church some fifty years or so after the crucifixion. The Christian community in Jerusalem in AD 66 had no part in the Jewish revolt; according to the tradition, which there is no good reason to doubt, they took a communal decision to leave for the Decapolis (Eus. *HE*3, 5, 3). During the next couple of centuries the Christians were no more politically quietist than anyone else outside the governing élite; indeed they take pride in outdoing the pagans in their exercise of their responsibility as citizens. Every writer, from Justin to Lactantius who touches the issue, with the sole exception of the obscenely and violently eccentric Julius Africanus, is uncompromisingly for nonviolence, though Tertullian and Origen, while insisting that loyalty to Christ is incompatible with violence, allow a relative justification of violent acts for good motives in pre-Christian days or among non-Christians. No Christian before the time of Constantine would think of joining the army, but from about AD 170 there are records of Christian converts in the armed forces. The Church did not lay upon them the obligation of a withdrawal which would have been desertion; it refused to accept them into full membership until their time of service was over. The tense days at the end of the third century in fact did see Christians contracting out of the army at the cost of their lives; one of them, Marcellus, said, 'I threw down my arms; it was not seemly that a Christian man, who renders military service to the Lord Christ, should render it by earthly injuries.'

From the time of Constantine the Church moved increasingly away from the insights of the New Testament. James Douglass in his admirable *The Non-Violent Cross* wrote: 'When Constantine raised the cross above his troops, he raised before the Christian Church the same temptation which Satan had set before Christ on the mountain with the sight of all the kingdoms of the world. And the Christian Church – for understandable reasons and without the critical perspective of 1,600 years – accepted Constantine's offer.' From that point the majority of Christians ceased to have a commitment to nonviolent methods of working out the way of Christian love. Between the eleventh and thirteenth centuries Christians were sponsoring and undertaking the Crusades, military expeditions for the recovery of the so-called Holy Places from Islam. The record of the nominally Christian nations across the centuries has hardly been peaceable; they have sometimes seemed closer to the God of battles than to the Christ on the cross. As J. C. Squire wrote in 1914:

> God heard the embattled nations sing and shout,
> 'Gott strafe England!' and 'God save the King!'
> God this, God that, and God the other thing –
> 'Good God!' said God, 'I've got my work cut out.'

To this outline four qualifications need to be made.

First, the Church has endeavoured, however ineffectually, to keep warfare under control. In the fourth century Ambrose, followed by Augustine, began to develop the doctrine of the 'just' war, which is being canvassed by some as a guide to the 'just' revolution and the 'just' use of violence generally. As developed by the theologians of the later Middle Ages, notably

Bellarmine, Suarez and Vitoria, the doctrine of the just war involved seven conditions: (i) it must be declared by lawful authority (a difficulty when applied to revolution); (ii) the cause must be just (but who can determine this, and in the sinful ambiguities of our human condition, what does it mean?); (iii) the belligerents should have a rightful intention to advance good or avoid evil; (iv) the war must be fought by proper means (it is ironic that the Second Lateran Council in 1139 banned the use of the crossbow as 'deadly and odious to God'); (v) war must be a last resort; (vi) the innocent shall be immune from direct attack (this was subject to varying interpretations; it was often taken to mean that civilians should not suffer death); (vii) the amount of violence shall not be disproportionate.

Secondly, throughout the Dark Ages penance was prescribed for shedding blood even in a just war. So in the Penitential of St. Egbert in about 750: 'If a man has brought death to another in open battle, or through necessity when recovering by force something belonging to his master, he is to fast for forty days.' Again, in the Penitential of Reginon of Crum, 150 years or so later: 'He who in an open war shall have killed a man shall do penance for forty days.'

Thirdly, there is a general consensus that the soldiers of Christ and servants of God may not engage in the shedding of blood. So the Synod of Ratisbon in 742 declared: 'We absolutely and in all circumstances forbid all God's servants to carry arms, to fight, and to march against an army or against an enemy.' This is typical of many such pronouncements by councils, synods and popes. It might seem a reassertion of the New Testament position, but it turns out that the soldiers of Christ who 'require no arms' are the clergy, bishops and priests.

Fourthly, from time to time in the history of the Church, sects, groups or individuals have appeared who have understood the way of Christ in terms of socially concerned nonviolent action. Such are the 'historic peace churches', the Society of Friends, the Mennonites, and the Church of the Brethren. Individuals who have chosen this way include Francis of Assisi, Erasmus, and, in our own day, Martin Luther King, Martin Niemöller, Helder Camara, Danilo Dolci, George MacLeod, Hildegard Goss-Mayr, to name but a few.

When the United Reformed Church in Britain, in response to a challenge from the World Council of Churches, called a commission on Nonviolent Action, it ensured that the membership was ecumenical (from Roman Catholic to Society of Friends), that it included Members of Parliament and a soldier, as well as theologians, ministers of religion and university teachers, and that only a small proportion of its members were pacifists, the majority holding some form of a 'just war' doctrine. But the doctrine of the just war affirms that war may be used only as a last resort, and the members of the commission, pacifist and non-pacifist alike, found that they had not remotely begun to explore the resources of nonviolent action or to approach its limits.

It must be repeated: the true Christian is a revolutionary, a nonviolent revolutionary. In *The Scottish Journal of Theology* for June 1968 the Czech theologian J. M. Lochman wrote well that

the testimony of non-violent love is not true if it is understood quietistically or ideologically (as a luxury-attitude in which the *beati possidentes* can indulge); it is true only if it is expressed in serious Christian testimony, i.e. in a revolutionary way, attacking the inhuman, godless structures of the world in the light of God's kingdom. It is only through ecumenical solidarity with the hungry, oppressed people in the developing countries, and by supporting their justified revolutionary demands, that the privileged Christians of Europe today can make a testimony of non-violent love which will carry any conviction.

It must be repeated too that Jesus does not offer those who follow him easy successes. Sometimes, as with the centurion at the cross, men's hearts will be moved, but often, as with the centurion, it is after the crucifixion. And it is better to be crucified as a danger to the comfortable established order than ignored as innocuous.

In fact we have seen the way in which active nonviolent

involvement can change a situation enough to recognise that, even humanly speaking, we have not begun to realise its potential.

In the lives of individuals we may recall how the monk Telemachus intervened to protest against the scandal of the gladiatorial 'shows' in Christian Rome, and was cut down among the jeers and plaudits of the cruel crowd, and how, beyond prediction or calculation, his witness led to the abolition of this form of murder for sport. We may recall how the American Quakers sat unarmed with open doors and found that the Indians laid aside their scalping tomahawks. We may remember how Sundar Singh, like Francis before him, walked with confidence among brigands and wild animals. We may think of the American Ned Richards after the first World War, going deliberately out of his sheltered life to Armenia and facing the marauding Kurds with unarmed love.

But it is not only in the lives of individuals, but of groups and nations too. In the nineteenth century the Hungarians, oppressed by Austria, rose in violent revolt under Kossuth, and were violently suppressed. Then Ferenc Deak showed a new lead, of nonviolent withdrawal of co-operation. It was a long, patient campaign lasting seventeen years, but it won lasting benefits. Passive resistance to Tsarist oppression in Finland at the start of this century achieved similar results. From New Zealand there is a remarkable story of the Maoris, now Christian, meeting English soldiers advancing for battle, with girls and children singing and dancing and offering garlands. From Brazil comes the extraordinary account of how the professional soldier, Candedo Rondon, ended centuries of war with the Indian tribes by giving his soldiers an absolute command 'Die if you must but kill never', probably the most unusual command ever given to an army. Some soldiers did die; one platoon was massacred; but Rondon refused reprisals, and won over the Indians by nonviolent suffering. Gandhi showed something of the potentiality of nonviolent methods in India. The story of the nonviolent work at Le Chambon-sur-Lignon under Nazi occupation shows something of the potentiality even in face of the most ruthless régimes.

Swomley in his book explores four case-studies in constructive revolution. One, comparatively little known over here, deals with the overthrow, by nonviolent means, of the brutal Guatemalan dictator, General Jorge Ubico ('I am like Hitler. I execute first and give trial afterwards.'). Others concern episodes in Chile in 1931 and El Salvador in 1944; in each case an oppressive government was brought down by strikes, boycotting and demonstrations, though only in Guatemala was there anything approaching a truly revolutionary situation. The final study, of Martin Luther King, shows a positive nonviolent liberation movement. In South Africa the turning of the liberation movement away from Albert Luthuli's nonviolence to violence was disastrous. The South African government knew well how to suppress violence; before the great nonviolent demonstration in Cape Town they had been uncertain and uneasy. So in the USA the Black Panthers turned impatiently away to violence, only to find pragmatically that violence achieved less than nonviolence, so that Bobby Seale transformed himself into a suave, cool, gentle, well-dressed, persuasive campaigner. The California grape-workers led by Cesar Chavez and the Sicilian peasants led by Danilo Dolci are other recent examples of corporate nonviolent challenges to oppression.

Ralph Waldo Emerson once wrote:

If you have a nation of men who have risen to that height of moral cultivation that they will not declare war or carry arms, for they have not so much madness left in their brains, you have a nation of benefactors, of true, great and able men. Let me know more of that nation. I shall not find them defenceless, with idle hands springing at their sides. I shall find them men of love, honour and truth – men of immense industry, men whose influence is felt to the end of the earth – men whose very look and voice carry the sentence of honour and shame, and all forces yield to their energy and persuasion.

Whenever we see the doctrines of peace embraced by a nation we may be assured it will not be one that invites injury but one, on the contrary, with a friend in the bottom of the heart of every man, even of the violent and the base, one against which no weapon can prosper, one which is looked upon as the asylum of the human race and has the blessings of mankind.

It would be good to think that Britain might be that nation, and have the courage to break through the deadlock caused by fear.

There is another way and a better way than violence. It is the way of Jesus. It is hard to see how people can profess faith in him while denying that nonviolent love has direct political relevance; hard to see how they can assert the centrality of the Cross to the Christian faith while denying its power in social conflict. Jürgen Moltmann has put it magnificently in *The Crucified God* (p. 248). 'Love can be crucified, but in crucifixion it finds its fulfilment and becomes love of the enemy. Thus its suffering proves to be stronger than hate.' Christ showed a new way of life, a way of changing the world. It was politically relevant. It was *in its own way* revolutionary. It was the way of love, the way of the Cross, the way of nonviolence, the way of Truth-force, Soul-force, Love-force. It is still the way. He seeks to fulfil it in us. The power is not ours but his.

The theme of the World Council of Churches Assembly in Nairobi was 'Jesus Christ frees and unites'. It is possible at once to free and unite only through nonviolent love.

9

Love God with all your mind: Education

> And one of the scribes came up and heard them disputing with one another, and seeing that he answered them well, asked him, 'Which commandment is the first of all?' Jesus answered, 'The first is, "Hear, O Israel: The Lord our God, the Lord is one; and you shall love the Lord your God with all your heart, and with all your soul, and with all your mind, and with all your strength." '
>
> Mark 12. 28–30

A Christian approach to education must start from a Christian view of society and of the individual. A theology of education is needed.

Make no mistake about it. Education matters. The great centralities of life are to be taught (Deut. 6.1–9). Further, we know from sources outside the Bible how insistent the Jews were that every child should grow up in mastery of a practical skill: so Jesus was trained as a carpenter, Paul as a tent-maker, Andrew and Peter as fishermen. It is true that Jesus teases Nicodemus about his academic standards which blind him to deeper truths (John 3.1–21), true too that the early church did not contain many 'wise after the flesh' (1 Cor. 1.26). But it is also true that it is Jesus who adds to the Deuteronomic commandment the injunction to love God with all the mind (Mark 12.30), and that he sends his followers out to teach (Matt. 28.20).

Education builds on the past, acts in the present, equips for the future. God is the Lord of History. The past is his. The inherited conglomerate which one generation transmits to its successors has been shaped by his Spirit. We cannot disown the past, even if we would. Nor should we. G. K. Chesterton once said that a sense of history was essential to true democracy, since it gave a vote to those who were dead and gone. But, willy-nilly, we are formed by the past. We are the product, but not the determined product, of our heredity and environment. We may accept it uncritically, we may rebel against it, we cannot escape from it. Harold Loukes said well of student protesters against their society that 'even when they rebel, even rebel radically, they rebel with the language and moral concepts and social tools they have learned in that society'. A theology of education is based upon a theology of history.

Education is related to the development of individuals, to the respect owed to a child as a person in his or her own right. As one of the great Puritans put it, 'no father should use his children at his own fantasy'; the child should be trained for the service of the commonwealth. But the state (whatever that may be), or the politicians and bureaucrats in power at any one time, should not identify themselves and their purposes with the service of the commonwealth; the state should not use its children at its own fantasy either. Education then is concerned with growing boys and girls, each with his own gifts, each with an immeasurable potential for good or evil, each formed in God's image, each with that image marred by forces from outside and forces from within. A theology of education is based upon a theology of the individual.

Education must also be related to the needs of society. It is largely paid for by society. It is related to the community, past, present and future. The service of the commonwealth is a wholly proper aim for those engaged in education to bear in mind. A theology of education is based upon a theology of the community.

Education was a major theme of some of the preparatory papers for the World Council of Churches' meeting in Nairobi in 1975. These preliminary explorations were analysed under three heads.

The first was the educative context. Education takes place within a given series of cultural, political and economic structures. As such it tends to perpetuate the *status quo*. But as

Christians we must assert that the image of God is not to be manipulated, or (in a phrase due to David Jenkins) we shall find ourselves from Black Paper to black gloom retreating instead of from glory to glory advancing. The educative context also includes social organisations of different kinds including the business community, the military establishment and the impact of the media. It further includes more intensively personal group experiences in (for example) family and church.

The result is an interaction of school and society to which insufficient attention is sometimes given. There is a constant tension between conformation and transformation. Sometimes, thank God, the school can repair the damage done by a poor home. Sometimes, thank God, the home can repair the damage done by a poor school. Sometimes, thank God, they pull together for good. Sometimes there is an alternating process. A girl may be encouraged to study until there is a family crisis, when she is expected to drop her books and take over.

There are other tensions. Education, conscious or unconscious, is around us all the time. A Puritan home may seek to divert a teenage boy's awareness of the female form, but a couple of minutes on a London Underground escalator will restore him to the facts of life. A school may suggest that the highest value lies in knowledge or service but there are many influences around him to suggest that it lies in money. So the formal structures of education and the informal influences of society interact.

Do we seek a competitive or co-operative society? What is the sort of education appropriate to each? Peter Lapwood, a boy of great promise, tragically cut off in a road accident, stayed with his family in communist China for some time after most Europeans had left. Eventually they returned to Britain, and he went to school in Cambridge. After a period he was asked to compare his experience of education in China and in England. He reflected and replied: 'In China they taught us to co-operate, here you teach us to compete. In China if anyone was floundering all the rest of us would join together to help them; here you call that cheating.' What effect on subsequent society does competition in school have? Equally is it right to send boys and girls out into a competitive world, when they have been trained only in the values of a co-operative society? And when the community as a whole is deeply divided between the values of competition and co-operation how can a school remain uncommitted? For the values as such are opposed to one another.

The second heading was 'Educational systems'. Here there is a difference to be noted between the sort of responsibility exercised by the Government and non-church agencies on the one hand, and churches on the other. Governmental schools over most of the world have had a tendency to encourage the emergence of an élite. They have had the curious, though not indefensible, purpose of segregating people from life in order to prepare them for life, and the prospective élite have welcomed this. Hence the 'ivory tower' university.

There is a curious example of this in Shakespeare's *Love's Labour Lost*. I used to think this a piece of entertaining froth. I now see underneath the froth a profound social philosophy. The king and his courtiers, notably the witty, brilliant Biron, shut themselves away from real life. Why? Because they want to play with words and ideas. They want to enjoy the newly discovered pattern of Renaissance education. Into that artificial retreat came the women, representing the real world. For a little they engage in 'games people play', and beat the men. Then, suddenly, dramatically, comes the messenger of death, and any producer of any competence shows this as the reassertion of the real world. The women withdraw into the real world to which they belong, and draw the men out of their ivory tower in following them. But this is not enough. The king is set to a year's practice of Zen or Yoga, Biron to a year working in a ghetto. It is incredibly contemporary. The real world is not in the educational retreat, but in the spiritual world and in the place where people are in need.

Tanzania in its public education has done something to restore the unity of education and its social context and to integrate life and learning with their maxim 'Every school a farm and every farm a school'. Maoist China has aimed at a similar pattern. The

Latin American educators Ivan Illich and Paolo Freire, have advocated 'deschooling society' precisely because schools have tended to take children away from real life. They argue for an education which starts where the child is, and heightens his consciousness of his environment; this is the process referred to by the ugly but convenient word 'conscientisation'.

The work of the churches in education was once to provide education for those who did not belong to the social élite. But the churches themselves have come to provide schools and colleges, which, being fee-paying, in the end support the rich not the needy. The Jesuits in Mexico City shut their traditional school for this reason, and used their resources where the real need lay.

Even when the churches are about their own business, as in the training of the clergy, the question must be asked whether such training for leadership may not of itself be deeply divisive, creating a gap between those so trained and the Christian community as a whole.

The essential work of Christian education is equipping the saints for the work of ministry. This will not be achieved by driving a wedge between the ministers and those to whom they minister. A representative of the Orthodox Church has said that 'Education first of all is participation in a community.'

The third section of the preparatory document is headed 'Learning for Liberation and Community'. The tone of the section is reflected in two final quotations. The first, from Taiwan, says 'Education is to develop and liberate the God-given potential for full human development in service to a just and open society.' The second, from Canada, says 'Education is to keep alive the hope and to experience the reality of human maturity and caring so that society may become more just and open and people more free.'

On the face of it both comments are allied to one side of the educational debate. To use a crude image, and one not to be pressed, is education an oilcan to keep the wheels turning smoothly, or a spanner in the works? Matthew Arnold drew an antithesis between a world already dead and a world powerless to be born. Education is the bridge between the old world and the new. But which is it to reflect? Oilcan or spanner?

There is no doubt that in the past and present the conscious direction of education has been towards conserving and reinforcing the values of existing society. Mill in his essay on Coleridge saw education as historically the principal means to that end, and that end as the chief object of education.

> To train the human being in the habit, and thence, the power of subordinating his personal impulses and aims, to what were considered the ends of society; of adhering, against all temptation, to the course of conduct which those ends prescribed; of controlling in himself all the feelings which were liable to militate against those ends, and encouraging all such as tended towards them; this was the purpose, to which every outward motive that the authority directing the system could command, and every inward power or principle which its knowledge of human nature enabled it to evoke, were endeavoured to be rendered instrumental.

Illich similarly offers a very subtle analysis for our own day when he speaks of the Myth of Unending Consumption which has taken the place of belief in life everlasting, and of the way in which schools encourage this by treating knowledge as a commodity in which they traffic.

Even the liberal university of Newman and Jowett was not quite as detached as its protagonists liked (in all sincerity) to think. The nineteenth-century British university was in fact offering an education appropriate to the Victorian ruling-class, and its products went out to govern vast tracts of Asia or Africa with Sophocles or Thucydides or Cicero or Horace under their pillow. Imperial Rome provided them with models and warnings, and their philosophy of life was taken from the ancient Stoics, tinged with Horace's urbane Epicureanism. The interesting part of Newman's analysis is that he argues from university to church. If he had argued the other way round he might have seen the university's function as not merely to rule (that is, negatively, to limit change by prescribing bounds) and to mediate, but also to prophesy.

Fortunately it is not as easy as this might imply. A spanner can be used to facilitate smooth running, an oilcan may be thrown into the works. A wise man once said 'Education is like ivory. You grab hold of a chunk of it – and find that attached is a whopping great beast that you don't know what to do with.' The education which is directed towards preserving the values of society has always succeeded in producing rebels against that society. Athenian education produced Plato. The Platonist education of the early Middle Ages produced Aquinas and the Aristotelian revolution, a revolution so dangerous that the exposition of Aristotle's works was banned in Paris. The Aristotelian education of the late Middle Ages produced the Renaissance scientists who knocked Aristotle off his pedestal. The liberal German university produced Karl Marx, and Clark Kerr's Berkeley produced Mario Savio.

The antithesis is not absolute. The priest and prophet are both needed, the priest who conserves and institutionalises, and in so doing fossilises the values of the past, and the prophet who proclaims the will of God for the present and for the future, but whose words are wasted in the empty air unless they can be brought somehow into the social order. We can never break with the past. The wheels of society do need oiling. Abraham Flexner offered a scathing indictment of the 'service-station' mentality of the American universities of the thirties; but as long as there are cars, there must be service-stations. We may or may not need theologians or lawyers, but we assuredly need doctors and engineers. We cannot follow Rousseau's formula of deciding what it is that we are now doing and then doing the exact opposite, like the mother in the *Punch* cartoon who said 'Go and see what Tommy's doing and tell him not to.' Flexner's dictum that the cardinal principle of the university should be irresponsibility is the merest epigram, designed to shock. Education cannot disown the past; but it must not be owned by it.

At much the same time there was fresh thinking going on in Unesco, which led to a 21-point programme.

1. Lifelong education should be the keystone of all educational policies in the years ahead, in industrially-developed as well as developing countries.

2. Lifelong education presupposes a complete reconstruction of education. Education must cease being confined within school walls. Education should become a true mass movement.

3. Education should be provided in many ways. What counts is not how a person has been educated, but what real knowledge he or she has gained.

4. Artificial or outdated barriers between different branches and levels of education and between formal and non-formal education should be abolished.

5. Education for pre-school-age children should be a major objective for educational strategies in the 1970s.

6. Millions of children and young persons are still deprived of education. Universal basic education, geared to national needs and resources, should be a priority objective of educational policies for the 1970s.

7. Rigid distinctions between different branches of education should be removed. Education, from primary and secondary levels, should have a combined theoretical, technological, practical and manual character.

8. Education should aim not only to train young people for specific jobs, but also equip them to adapt to a variety of occupations.

9. Responsibility for technical training should not fall exclusively on the school system. It should be shared by schools, business, industry and out-of-school education.

10. Higher education should be expanded and made varied enough to meet individual and community needs. Traditional attitudes towards the university must change.

11. Access to different types of education and employment should depend only on a person's knowledge, capacities and aptitudes.

12. Development of adult education in and out of school, should

be a priority objective of educational strategies during the next ten years.

13. All literacy teaching should be geared to a country's objectives in social and economic development.

14. Aids to self-education, including language laboratories, libraries, data banks, and audio-visual equipment, should be integrated into all education systems.

15. Education systems should be conceived and planned in terms of possibilities offered by new educational techniques.

16. Teacher training programmes should make full use of the latest teaching aids and methods.

17. All hierarchical differences among teachers in primary schools, technical colleges, secondary schools and universities should be abolished.

18. Teachers should be trained to be educators rather than specialists in the transmission of knowledge.

19. Skilled auxiliaries from the trades and professions (workers, technicians and executives) should be brought in to teach in schools. Students should also participate, educating themselves while teaching others.

20. Contrary to traditional practice, teaching should adapt itself to the learner. The student should have greater freedom to decide for himself what he wants to learn and how and where to learn it.

21. Students and the public as a whole should be given a greater say in decisions affecting education.

If we accept our earlier analysis that we as Christians are seeking an Open Society, certain principles follow for education.

First, we must not be afraid of change. F. M. Cornford in *Microcosmographia Academica* laid down with deadly satire the Principle of Dangerous Precedent: 'You should not now do an admittedly right action for fear you, or your equally timid successors, should not have the courage to do right in some future case, which *ex hypothesi*, is essentially different, but superficially resembles the present one. Every public action which is not customary, either is wrong, or, if it is right, is a dangerous precedent. It follows that nothing should even be done for the first time.'

On the contrary, we must prepare for change. Willy-nilly, the world is changing and we must fit people for a changing world. And this is theologically right. That ultimate reality is static was, as we have seen, the view of Plato in his middle age only, not that of Jesus at all. Despite the hymn-writer, change is not synonymous with decay. One doubts whether the disciples called Jesus 'Thou who changest not', Jesus who was forever startling them with the unexpected. Christians believe in a dynamic reality, a living God.

Education must be flexible. There may be some wrongs in education, but there are precious few rights which can be taken from one solution and applied to another with certainty and without qualification. This is one of the problems of a state-system of education. Such a system is inevitably standardised; it exists to maintain standards. But education must be free, flexible, experimental. Whether or not one approves in detail of his views, there must be room for an A. S. Neill within the educational network. Comprehensive schools are purposed to bring into the educational system values which were neglected before. But it is important to ask whether those very values can be maintained when schools rise above a certain number (seemingly about 750), when the result is a single school serving a vast area with no other parallel school for miles around; whether those values are cherished in a formal amalgamation of two or three sets of buildings a mile or two apart, or when the amalgamation of two schools leads to a less diversified curriculum with less choice than either school offered before; whether the values of the comprehensive principle always outweigh other values, such as the value of tradition; whether an experiment in some areas with giving the secondary modern schools more resources than the grammar schools might have produced interesting results. This is not to attack the comprehensive principle; it is to suggest that a wider experimentalism might be no bad thing. That great and eccentric Christian Tolstoy said that 'the only method of education is experiment, and its only criterion freedom'.

Secondly, authoritarian attitudes are not appropriate to the Open Society and they are not appropriate to the education designed to lead up to it. It has been amply shown that an authoritarian attitude to education and authoritarian attitudes to society go together; it has also been shown that schools which practise repressive discipline suffer severe defacement of their lavatory walls. There is here a problem. For we do seek to encourage students to recognise the authority of the truth. But this is not the same as the authority of the teacher however expert. Indeed it is a great saying of Jesus that 'the truth shall set you free' (John 8.32). It is the key to the twofold rôle of education in conserving and transforming, for if we are dedicated to the truth we shall conserve it when we find it, as infinitely precious, and use it as a sword to slice away the falsehood of the past.

Thirdly, education should encourage conscientisation, a sensitive awareness of the needs of the community around us, and a determination to do something about them. Even when school or college is detached from its environment it is possible to reach out into society. The knight can sally forth from his ivory tower on a dragon-slaying expedition. And within the tower there can be a mirror on the world like the Lady of Shalott's. Scientists can be aware of the interaction of science and society, and of the social responsibility of the scientist. Even as a remote classicist I have found strangely relevant things happening: Plato's *Republic* in its identification of corruption and nepotism as the two great ills of society suddenly illuminating the Nigeria of 1965–6, or Euripides's anti-war plays speaking to the consciousness and conscience of American students during the Vietnam war. And theology and religious studies should always be fostering such conscientisation.

Fourthly, students, whether in school or college, must have the opportunity of finding, forming, changing and deepening their life styles. Each must find his self-image, work out his rational morality, nurture the movement from external command to internal stance. If they do not do so now, the odds are that they never will, and that they will be left to the mercy of irrational prejudice from within, authoritarianism from without, and vague habits of behaviour. Not least is this true in religious education. We have moved far in the last few years, from religious instruction to religious education, even further since my own schooldays when the period, even in the sixth form, was baldly labelled 'Scripture'. At a multi-faith conference at Leicester a few years ago which I had the joy of chairing, an unanimous statement was agreed by Christians (both Catholic and Protestant), Jews, Muslims, Hindus, Sikhs, Buddhists and Humanists. It declared that religious education is an essential part of all education. Its function is to open to growing boys and girls awareness of the religious dimension, and of the existence of religions (the plural is important), and to help them to discover their own life style. Christ does not constrain our allegiance; nor should we seek to constrain the allegiance of others. Religion cannot be forced, said Thomas à Kempis; there is nothing so free as religion.

What this is about is wisdom. Solomon was commended in his dream because he asked for the gift of wisdom (1 Kings 3.5–15). Wisdom is the power of discernment. It starts from the fear of the lord (Psalm 111.10; Job 28.28; Prov. 1.7; 9.10); it means turning aside from evil (Job 28.28; Prov. 8.13; 16.6). In the later Old Testament and the Apocrypha there are four great hymns to Wisdom: Job 28.12–28; Proverbs 8.1–9.6; Ecclesiasticus 24; Wisdom of Solomon 7–8. Wisdom comes from God and is seen seated at God's side, God's companion. At the same time Wisdom is a teacher of men. So in the New Testament James says that the man of knowledge should show in practice a good conversation laced with meekness of wisdom.

Tennyson has it well.

> Our little systems have their day;
> They have their day and cease to be:
> They are but broken lights of Thee,
> And Thou, O Lord, art more than they ...

Let knowledge grow from more to more,
　But more of reverence in us dwell;
　That mind and soul, according well,
May make one music as before,

　　But vaster.
But vaster.

10

Up to the hill of the Lord: The way forward

Who shall climb up to the hill of the Lord?
And who shall stand in his holy place?
He who has clean hands and a pure heart,
who does not lift up his soul to what is false,
and does not swear deceitfully.
He will receive blessing from the Lord,
and vindication from the God of his salvation.
Such is the generation of those who seek him,
who seek the face of the God of Jacob.

Psalm 24.3–6

On 18th October, 1975, the Archbishop of Canterbury held a Press Conference at which he delivered a message to the nation.

I want to speak not only to members of the churches, but to all those who are concerned for the welfare of our nation at a time when many thoughtful people feel that we are drifting towards chaos. Many are realising that a materialistic answer is no real answer at all. There are moral and spiritual issues at stake. I believe the only creed that makes sense is: 'God first – Others next – Self last.' I see this worked out in the person and teaching of Jesus Christ. He has shown us the way – He gives us the power to follow it.

Dr. Coggan insisted on the importance of the individual. Each man and woman matters. The family matters. Good work matters. Attitudes matter. We have been thinking too much about money, and greed and envy have been leading us to chaos. An American politician said that Britain had lost an empire and not found a rôle. Rather has Britain lost an empire and not found her soul.

At much the same time the British Council of Churches was involved in a major exploration of the theme 'Christian hope for our time'. The title was not entirely happy. Of the three theological virtues, as love is the greatest, so hope is the least, for it depends wholly on love and faith. 'All my hope on God is founded,' says the hymn, and Christians have no light word of encouragement to those in crisis. This was made amply clear in the course of a survey in which some two hundred or so people were asked about the principal issues facing the nation. The mood revealed by the enquiry was a sombre one; it produced a picture of 'insecurity and anxiety verging on fear, disillusionment and tiredness bordering on hopelessness, perplexity and bewilderment leading to a sense of powerlessness'. There were personal fears associated with lack of security. Here was a sense of fading and failing ideals, and a general retreat from politics. Yet many of the problems identified were political and economic. Most people feel remote from the centres of power, and the gulf between the powerful and powerless is growing rather than diminishing; bureaucracy actually increases the mystique of those in positions of authority. Meantime problems like inflation, unemployment, the poverty gap, growth economics, keeping up with the Joneses, pollution and conservation are oppressive. So are a number of social problems, particularly violence, the lack of any real sense of community, and the absence of agreed moral standards. A strong desire for great reforms was coupled to an equal desire to preserve precious inheritance. There was a longing for a better society and a fear of things falling apart. There was a general sense of spiritual crisis, of a shortage of Christian leadership, and an absence of prophetic insight. The church itself is soft, acquiescent in the confused spirit of the age, and disinclined to take seriously its own foundations. It is significant that not merely is there an absence of effective belief in the Holy Spirit, the active presence of God among us, in all but a few Pentecostal churches, but not a single respondent mentioned this or commented upon it.

Reflection on this afterwards, and on the discussions in the Assembly alike in groups and in plenary session led to a list of ten areas of exploration: Britain in a World Setting; World Justice and Economic Priorities; Power and Powerlessness; Law, Order, Freedom and Human Rights; Employment and Unemployment; Creating Community; Violence, Nonviolence and Social Change; Culture, Morality and Styles of Life; Leadership and Authority; Education and Society.

It is essential that all these topics, huge and daunting as they are, be opened up in a variety of ways and at all levels. This is so important that I must give a number of examples. There is need for some fresh examination of the economic rôle of Britain in the late twentieth and perhaps even the early twenty-first century. Certain points are obvious enough; yet it is not clear that they have been properly weighed.

Food supply comes first; without that nothing can be done. What proportion of our food can we produce ourselves? Are we developing our food industry at the expense of the Third World (through the extravagant use of protein in feeding animals, for instance)? What food do we need to import? Can we reduce this by a relatively simple change in our eating habits? If so, how can we encourage the change? Can we concentrate on imports from the Third World (sugar, fruit, cocoa, groundnuts, etc.) in such a way as will be mutually beneficial to them and to us? Food from abroad must be paid for: what are the goods and services which are needed in the areas from which the food will come, and which we are best in a position to provide? This begins to set one pattern for industry.

Next, what natural resources have we? North Sea oil! All hope is pinned on that. Let us be careful not to become dependent on a natural resource in such a way that we swiftly exploit and exhaust it; let us see that it is used constructively, and not just to enable even more private cars to clog up the road and pollute the atmosphere. Have we really made the most of the great potential of Scotland and Wales, two somewhat neglected areas, for the growing of forests and the production of wood? What part do, can and should our historic monuments play in our economy? They attract millions of tourists to Britain. If this is a major concern, certain conclusions follow, as that we ought to put more public money into their preservation, we ought to reduce pollution which destroys them, and we ought to improve communications.

Next, what industries is Britain best equipped to support? Perhaps, there is no answer to this, and the particular industries which have developed may be a matter of historical accident, though equally plainly Britain is a more natural base for a ship-building industry than is Switzerland! But even if industries have arisen from historical accident, they have become a matter of tradition and accumulated expertise, which should not lightly be discarded; at the same time the stream of history flows past, and there is no sense in propping up a historical industry which has ceased to serve its purpose; as well insist on maintaining the manufacture of crossbows and handploughs. But this in turn means that there is need for the transformation to other purposes of industries which have outlined their usefulness, or the development of new industries in the same area, or for greater mobility (which may be socially undesirable).

What are Britain's assets? It is sometimes said that Britain's prime asset lies in inventiveness. Is this so? If it is, is it not vital to be open to new forms of industry and to a considerable measure of experiment? And do our emergent patterns of education encourage such inventiveness? Would a pattern of education which did so cut across other important values? What place ought advertising to have in the economy? It is no doubt in some sense necessary. But can we afford that part of it which encourages the purchase of luxury goods? 'You Self-indulgent, Tight-fisted, Modern Living, Comfort Lover You . . . Don't you really love unashamed luxury?' asked one ad. What place should the pools have? A popular pastime which clogs up (and supports) the GPO, but is unproductive?

It would be possible to go on. These are huge questions. They are possibly naive, because they are inexpert. They are questions which must be answered by experts who are also Christians, because they involve both technical knowledge and judgements of value. But it would be worth being in this way both realistic and Utopian – Utopian because it means spelling out a non-existent state, realistic because it is the only way to an economy which makes any sense. If we could draw up a picture of a sane society, further questions follow. How do we, how can we travel from A to B, from here to there? How can such a movement command assent? And, with cold calculation, in a plural society, where many people will be doing many things, good things out of selfish motives, bad things out of selfish motives, stupid things out of worthy motives, good things out of worthy motives (for the most part) mixed things out of mixed motives – what are the vital steps?

At the same time there is need for local groups to be asking questions about power and powerlessness as it affects them, about questions of law, order, freedom and human rights as they have emerged in the local situation; about their own problems of employment and unemployment, about their own cultures, moralities and styles of life, about the education offered in their local schools and its relation to the society of which they are members. If the Church is really the Church, then these discussions can take place within the particular Christian fellowships. If the Church is composed predominantly of whites, middle-class, middle-aged, and with little risk of unemployment, it will be necessary to draw in others. This might even be a step to revivifying the Church! But it is also important that the Christians continually test their thinking against the New Testament and the way of Christ, and are continually open to new guidance from the Holy Spirit. Important too is the concept of a 'study-action' group. People are today understandably impatient with the old-fashioned study group which ended with worthy verbiage. The final question becomes not 'What do you think about . . . ?' but 'What are you going to do about . . . ?'

So there is a wide variety of questions which can and must be asked. What is the theology which undergirds the Christian's launching into society? What is the sort of society we seek? What structures would enable such a society to emerge? What changes would this mean? What might be a single key change? What changes would this mean in my own locality? What must I do about it? What changes would it mean in the life of my local church? What sort of people will form this society? What changes does this mean in me?

There is a wide variety of ways in which answers can be pursued, through high-powered national committees, through the internal programmes of the churches, through individuals charged with the challenge, through councils of churches in some of the larger cities, through Christian groups in schools and colleges, through local churches and groups within them.

There is a wide variety of ways in which conclusions may emerge. There may be recommendations, general or detailed, which can be discussed with the government, the Trades Unions, the CBI and similar bodies. They may be developed in publications, communicated to the press, disseminated through the news-media. There may be considerable changes in the life of the churches. There may be local action, local pressures local changes. There may be changes in the lives of individuals.

In his Eddington lectures Sir Joseph Hutchinson called for a return to Jesus. Jesus had his priorities right. The most important thing is to change the goals of our society. Those who met in the dark days of December 1914 to form the Fellowship of Reconciliation affirmed that they were called to a life-service for the enthronement of Love in personal, commercial and national life, and that the Power, Wisdom and Love of God stretch far beyond the limits of our present experience, and that he is ever waiting to break forth into human life in new and larger ways. Twenty-five years ago a wise Indian Christian said to me of us British Christians: 'You think far too much about your traditions and not enough about your destiny.' It is still true.

Something of the yearning which lies behind this appears in a poem from Nigeria, written by Amba Oduyoye on the Sunday after St. Luke's Day, 20th October, 1974.

REFLECTION ON WHOLENESS

Busy, normal people: the world is here.

Can you hear it wailing, crying, whispering?

Listen: the world is here –

Don't you hear it.

Praying and sighing and groaning for wholeness?

Sighing and whispering: wholeness, wholeness, wholeness?

An arduous, tiresome, difficult journey towards wholeness.

God, who gives us strength of body, Make us whole.

Wholeness of persons: well-being of individuals.

The cry for bodily health and spiritual strength is echoed from
person to person, from patient to doctor.

It goes out from a soul to its pastor.

We, busy, 'normal' people: we are sick.

We yearn to experience wholeness in our innermost being;

In health and prosperity, we continue to feel un-well,

Un-fulfilled, or half-filled.

There is a hollowness in our pretended well-being:

Our spirits cry out for the well-being of the whole human
family.

We pride ourselves in our traditional communal ideology, our
extended family.

The beggars and the mad people in our streets:
  – Where are their relatives?

Who is their father? Where is their mother?

We cry for the wholeness of humanity.

But the liturgy of brokenness is without end.

Black and white;

Rich and poor;

Hausa and Yoruba;

Presbyterian and Roman Catholic:

We are all parts of each other,

We yearn to be folded into the fulness of life – together.

Life, together with the outcast,
  The Prisoner, the mad woman, the abandoned child;

Our wholeness is intertwined with their hurt.

Wholeness means healing the hurt,
Working with Christ to heal the hurt,
Seeing and feeling the suffering of others,
Standing alongside them.
Their loss of dignity is not their loss:
It is the loss of our human dignity,
We busy, 'normal' people.
The person next to you: with a different language and culture.
With a different skin or hair colour –
It is God's diversity, making an unbroken rainbow circle –
Our covenant of peace with God, encircling the whole of
    humanity.
Christians have to re-enact the miracle of Good Friday:
The torn veil, the broken walls, the bridge over the chasm,
The broken wall of hostility between the Jew and the gentile.
The wall between the sacred and secular?
There is no wall
There is only God at work in the whole.
    Heal the sores on the feet.
    Salvage the disintegrated personality.
    Bind the person back into the whole.
For without that one, we do not have a whole:
    Even if there are ninety-nine:
    Without that one, we do not have a whole.
    God, who gives us strength of body, Make us whole.

In the end the change will come from changed individuals.
When Jesus began his preaching with the word 'Repent', he was
not hoping for the comfortable feeling of guilt and the lump in
the throat which so many of us associate with the idea of repentance. He was not speaking of anything to do with the emotions
at all. He was saying, 'Turn round and face the other way';
'Change your thinking'; 'Your values are wrong; discard them
and acquire new ones'; 'Change your life-style'; 'Start the revolution in yourself'. When Malvolio picks up Maria's letter he
finds, 'When this you read, revolve.' Those words should be

emblazoned on our gospels, for they mean, 'When this you read, start a revolution – start with yourself, but don't finish there.'

So we note with encouragement, some of the revolutions which have been started. Life Style, for example.

Life Style is about –

1. Living more simply that others may simply live; recognising that our greed denies another's need; criticising our own life style before we criticise that of others.

2. Deciding what to buy, how much to spend and what to do without in the light of the urgent need to conserve the earth's resources and to distribute them more fairly.

3. Not being led on by advertisements into buying what we do not in fact want; taking what opportunities we can of challenging wasteful packaging and 'built-in obsolescence'.

4. Deciding on what percentage of our net disposable income we are going to give away for the benefit of those in need (especially in the developing continents of Asia, Africa and South America), making the amount so shared a first charge on our annual, monthly or weekly budget of expenditure.

5. Deciding whether regularly to do without a meal and to give to the hungry the money so saved; being generous without showing off and hospitable without extravagance.

6. Recognising that, like the sabbath, Life Style is made for us and not we for it; a style rather than a code; not a substitute for political or economic action but in many cases a springboard for such action; unashamedly Christian in origin but, or rather therefore, so worded as to be open to adherents of any creed or none; open also to those whose own poverty exempts from them from some of its provisions.

This is only one example of a widespread concern. At the Church Leaders' Conference called by the British Council of Churches in 1972 one of the commissions produced a challenge to all Christians:

TOWARDS SIMPLICITY OF LIFE

1. *See yourself as a citizen of the planet*
Questions of poverty and environment are distorted if seen only in local or national terms. (That is a point I have frequently made above.)

2. *Waste-watching*
Where you have a choice
   resist obsolescence; choose the longer lasting
   support public transport with your feet and your vote
   question advertisement
   resist wasteful packaging.

3. *Question your own life-style – not your neighbour's!*

4. *If possible, work out your way of life with the help of a group (family, friends, congregation)*
Asking such questions as:

   How can we measure our real needs (by the standards of our neighbours or by the needs of the poor)?

   How can we be joyful without being greedy or flamboyant (e.g. in hospitality)?

   How far does our personal way of life depend on *society's* wealth? Can our society's way of life be simpler? Is there any such change we ourselves can work for?

   How can we be good stewards without being over-scrupulous? What decisions about personal life are the decisive ones to make (e.g. budgeting; family size)?

   How can others benefit from what we have (our home, our car and other possessions)?

5. *Points to ponder*
   Happiness is knowing what I can do without
   My greed is another's need
   Am I detached from worldly goods if I keep what I have and want to add to them?

As Sir Joseph Hutchinson excellently put it: 'Simplicity of life style has a long history of commendation as a minor virtue. It has been drowned in the plenty of the last two decades. The plenty is ebbing away and simplicity may be forced upon us. Let us remember that it is a virtue.'

Another important movement in this area has been the move towards sharing, towards community life and collective responsibility. The Fellowship of Reconciliation 'Collective' referred to earlier will serve as an example. It is too early to say how it will work out. But we can see the reasons which have brought them together. They bear equal responsibility for their success or failure and have an equal stake in their effectiveness. Blame or achievement draws them closer together as people or as co-workers. The boring and exciting work can be shared out equally, and in emergencies they can step into one another's shoes. Living together is a test of the openness they are seeking for society as a whole. They have taken part-time jobs outside the Collective to avoid becoming like a set of ingrowing toenails; but basically they suffer no alienating split between 'work' and 'leisure'. They are seeking a lifestyle which will express the wholeness of their Christian commitment, a commitment to Christ's way of non-violent love; that lifestyle will be rooted in worship, in celebration; they aim at a heightened sense of communion, with self, with one another, with their fellow human beings, with the earth, with God.

There is need for a new evangelism. It will start from individuals but it will embrace society. The change in individuals must have its effect in the change of society. I have attempted to spell out this call in the following eight points:

1. We affirm the Lordship of Christ over all life.
2. We affirm the Lordship of Christ over our human societies.
3. We affirm the power of the Holy Spirit active among us.
4. As we read the Bible we find a word spoken alike to individuals and societies, to David and to Israel, to Paul and to the New Israel, a word which extends in judgement and compassion to Moab or Rome.
5. We must seek the way of life to which He calls us, alike as

individuals, within the *koinonia* of the Church, and in the wider society of which Christians are a part.

6. We can identify five major tasks to which God calls us in society:

(a) sharing

(b) caring, especially for the underprivileged

(c) reconciliation and the breaking of the barriers

(d) social justice

(e) *shalom*, which means wholeness, completeness.

7. We can identify some of those social evils which stand under Christ's judgement:

(a) love of money, possession by riches

(b) oppression and social injustice

(c) violence

(d) social divisiveness.

8. Our task is

(a) to call men and women to accept the Lordship of Christ as alone giving true purpose to their personal and social life

(b) to work out within the fellowship of committed Christians how we can realise the life in Christ

(c) to witness within society to a better and truer way.

For discussion and action

1. GOD'S CALL TO SOCIETY

1. What does it mean to say that God calls our nation?
2. How should the corporate life of the Church reflect its standing as the New Israel?
3. With a concordance look up the New Testament references to the Son of Man and discuss where it is meaningful to think of him as referring to 'the new humanity formed of Jesus and those who put on new life in and through him' (p. 16).
4. What are the structures which will make possible the emergence of the sort of society we want and will help to produce the sort of people who will make that society? (p. 18).

2. SHARING

1. What is the relevance of the teaching of Jesus to twentieth-century economy?
2. What is the relevance of Acts 4.32 (i) within the Church and (ii) within a wider, nominally Christian state?
3. Look carefully at what is said about the Scott Bader Commonwealth (pp. 29–31). Does this succeed in incorporating anything of the way of Jesus? Could it be improved? Could it be applied more widely?
4. If it could be shown that appealing to people's acquisitive desires would really raise the standard of living for everyone, would it be right to encourage this?

3. CARING

1. Consider the needs in your locality and work out a programme

in which your church or group, preferably with others, can share in meeting these.

2. Work out ways in which you can keep yourselves informed about world needs (e.g. each take a topic and keep up to date with it). Then write jointly as a group to Christians of the appropriate Minister or to your MP from time to time to express your Christian concern.

3. Hold a prayer meeting in which every concern you lift up to God has been carefully and informatively prepared. Let your prayers hold up real people in real situations. Be open that God's response may be a call to you to do something.

4. WORK

1. Does the so-called Protestant ethic (p. 45) contain any Christian insight?

2. Why should any Christian *want* to have more money than another? (p. 45).

3. What should we as a community do about dull jobs? Unpleasant jobs?

5. CONSERVATION

1. If the earth is the Lord's, what are our duties and responsibilities towards it?

2. Look at the last paragraph (pp. 67–8). What can your church or group do similarly?

6. DECENTRALISATION

1. Read together Romans 12.4–18; 1 Corinthians 12.4–31; Ephesians 4.4–16. Think how it changes the life of your church or group to take this seriously.

2. Does the Scott Bader pattern reflect Christian values? Could their experience be more widely applied?

3. Is small beautiful?

7. THE OPEN SOCIETY

1. What difference does it make to believe in the living God, the living Jesus, the living Spirit?

2. What about Christ and culture (p. 87)? Does Christ call us, when we turn to him, to turn away from the culture in which we were brought up, to accept it without change, or what? Let this be a practical discussion: what changes, if any, is it going to make to your life?

3. Is your church or group a really open society? What barriers might people feel to prevent them coming more fully in? What are you going to do about it?

4. How can we have a sounder partnership between women and men in our country, in your church, in the work and leisure activities you know?

8. NONVIOLENCE

1. Read Matthew 5.1–16; 38–48; 26.51–2; Romans 12.17–13.10 (remember the chapter division is not Paul's; the letter should be read continuously). How should Christians meet violence and oppression? Think of other passages. (All relevant passages are discussed in J. Ferguson *The Politics of Love*.)

2. Is the teaching of the New Testament relevant to the very different world of the twentieth century?

3. Individual Christians are called to love their enemies. Is it meaningful to speak of a nation loving its enemies?

9. EDUCATION

1. Education – for what?

2. What are the effects of (i) competition and (ii) authoritarianism in education?

3. If religious education in the schools were no longer directly Christian, how would the life and work of the churches have to change?

1. Pick out and discuss some of the questions on pp. 118–120.
2. Discuss the principles of Life Style (p. 129) and the statement 'Towards Simplicity of Life' (p. 130).
3. Are the eight points with which the book ends (pp. 131–2) a just statement of the call of Jesus Christ to men in their communal living?
3. Is yours a study-action group (p. 125)? What are you going to *do*?

Bibliography

Bergson, H., *The Two Sources of Religion and Morality*, E.T., New York: Henry Holt, 1935

Carson, R., *Silent Spring*, London: Hamish Hamilton, 1962

Chesterton, G. K., *The Napoleon of Notting Hill*, London: Bodley Head, 1904

Chesterton, G. K., *Autobiography*, London: Burns, Oates and Washbourne 1936, Hutchinson, 1969

Cornford, F. M., *Microcosmographia Academica*, Cambridge: Bowes and Bowes, 1949

Douglass, J., *The Non-Violent Cross*, London: Collier-Macmillan, 1969

Ehrlich, P., *The World's Children*

Emerson, R. W., *The Works of Ralph Waldo Emerson*, London: Routledge, 1904

Ferguson, J., *The Politics of Love*, Cambridge: James Clarke, n.d.

Hole, S. R., *Then and Now*, London: Hutchinson, 1901

Hutchinson, Sir Joseph, *The Challenge of the Third World*, Cambridge: CUP, 1975

Illich, I., *Deschooling Society*, London: Penguin, 1971

Meadows, D., and others, *The Limits to Growth*, London: Angus and Robertson, 1972

Mesarovic, M., and Pestel, E., *Mankind at the Turning-Point*, London: Hutchinson, 1975

Mill, J. S., *Dissertations and Discussions*, London: Routledge, n.d.

Moltmann, J., *The Crucified God*, London: SCM, 1974

Mumford, Lewis, *The City in History*, London: Pelican, 1966

Nicholson, Max, *The Environmental Revolution*, London: Hodder, 1969

Niebuhr, H. R., *Christ and Culture*, New York: Harper and Row, 1951

Oman, J., *The Natural and the Supernatural*, Cambridge: CUP, 1931

Osborn, Fairfield, *Our Plundered Planet*, London: Faber, 1948

Raven, C. E., *The Gospel and the Church*, London: Hodder & Stoughton, 1939

Roberts, M., *The Estate of Man*, London: Faber, 1951

Sayers, D. L., *Four Sacred Plays*, London: Gollancz, 1948

Schumacher, E. F., *Small is Beautiful*, London: Bland Briggs, 1973
Squire, J. C., *The Survival of the Fittest*, London: Allen and Unwin, 1916
Tawney, R. H., *Religion and the Rise of Capitalism*, London: Pelican, 1938
Temple, W., *Readings in St. John's Gospel*, London: Macmillan, 1945
Tennyson, A., *The Works of Alfred, Lord Tennyson*, London: Macmillan, 1890
Toynbee, A. J., *A Study of History*, London: OUP, 1963
Turgeniev, I., *Dream Tales and Prose Poems*, tr. C. Garnett, London: Heinemann, 1906
Vogt, W., *Road to Survival*, London: Gollancz, 1949
Weber, Max, *The Sociology of Religion*, London: Methuen, 1965
Wilson, Rev. H. O., 'The Christian and the World Around', *Reconciliation Quarterly*, I.I. (1971), pp. 18–22

Index of biblical passages

Genesis
1.1 82
1.26–7 9, 88, 94
1.31 12, 55
2.15 55
2.19–20 55
4.9 80
11.31 11

Exodus
3.10 11

Leviticus
25 20, 77

Numbers
22.30 84

Deuteronomy
6.1–9 108
6.21 12

1 Samuel
3.2–14 11

1 Kings
3.5–15 119
4.25 71

Job
28.12–28 111

Psalms
24.1–2 55
24.3–6 121
50.7 11
84.3 65
103.1–5 12
104.1–4 12
111.10 111

Proverbs
1.7 111
6.6 46
8.1–9.6 111
9.10 111
12.24 46
16.3 53
16.6 111

Isaiah
5.8 21
11.6–7 61
40.15 12
40.22 12
40.28 12
42.1–4 16
49.1–6 16
50.4–9 16
52.13–53.12 16
61.1–2 21
64.6 85

Jeremiah
1.5 11
20.7–9 11, 28
31.31 14

Ezekiel
17.24 73

Daniel
7.13 16

Hosea
2.8 82
2.18 65
7.10–11 14

Amos
2.1 13
7.2 73
9.7 13, 82

Jonah
3.10–4.1 28

Micah
2.2 21

Zechariah
3.10 71
4.6 69
4.10 23
9.9–10 14, 100

The Wisdom of Solomon
7–8 111

Ecclesiasticus
24 111

Matthew
5.1–7.28 15
5.1–16 135
5.5 65
5.38–48 135
5.41 101
5.45 22, 84, 101
6.9 82
6.19–24 22
6.24 29, 44
6.28 12, 65
7.21 125
10.8 22, 46
10.29 12, 65, 66
12.30 46
18.22 37
20.1–16 22
21.1–7 100
23.12 65
24.45 85
25.14–30 50
25.31–46 15, 32, 96
26.47 83
26.51–2 96, 101, 135
26.59–65 83
28.19–20 85, 108

Mark
1.15 21, 28, 128
1.16–20 11
2.5 11
2.14 11
2.27 129
4.26–9 22
8.33–4 100
9.2–8 84
10.19 15
10.21 22
10.23 22
10.45 48
12.26–7 82
12.28–31 71, 84, 90, 108

Luke
4.1–13 84, 100
4.18–19 21
5.24 44
6.24 22
10.30–37 36, 125
10.38–42 47
12.14 84
14.13 22
15.3–10 12
15.11–32 12, 23
16.1–9 55
16.19–21 22
19.8–9 11, 22
23.33 84
23.47 104

John
1.12 58, 85
1.14 83
3.1–21 108
3.8 84
5.17 44
8.11 11
8.32 118
14.19 83
15.12 26

Acts
2.9–11 85
4.31–3 20, 23

9.4 11
11.26–30 32

Romans
6.4–8 24
8 24, 83
12–13 100, 134–5
12.13 24

1 Corinthians
1.9 23–4
1.26 108
1.28 73
12.12–31 50, 73, 85, 127, 134
13.13 122
14.15 41

2 Corinthians
8.10–15 25
8.23 24

Galatians
3.8–14 88
3.28 80, 88
5.22 84

Ephesians
2.14 92, 128
4.4–16 50, 73, 134
4.13 16

Philippians
4.14–15 24

Colossians
1.24 24

2 Thessalonians
3.6–12 46

Philemon
17 24

Hebrews
10.31 82, 117
13.20 12–13

James
3.13 119

1 Peter
3.18 44

1 John
4.8 26, 82, 84
4.10–11 26, 71, 84
4.18 97
4.20 26

Revelation
21.4 44
21.5 82

General Index

Abelard, 87
acquisitiveness, 21, 122, 129
Acton, Lord, 69
Adam, 44
advertising, 39, 52, 124, 129, 130
aged, care of, 33
agriculture, 47–8, 65–6
ahimsa (non-harming), 66
aid, development, 38–9, 42–3
airport expansion, 72
à Kempis, Thomas, 119

Ambrose, 102
Anstey, Roger, 33
apostasy, 13
aptitudes, 49–50
Aquinas, Thomas, 87, 114
Aristotle, 114
arms, expenditure on, 96
Arnold, Matthew, 112–13
Athens, 72, 88, 114
Atonement, Day of, 20–21
Augustine, 87, 102
automation, 49
authoritarianism, 118–19
axioms, middle, 18–19

barriers, breaking of, 88, 90–95, 115, 132
Bergson, Henri, 80–81
Bonhoeffer, Dietrich, 99
Brandt, Willy, 40
Brazil, 38, 105
Briejer, Dr. J., 65, 66
Britain, official policy of 38–9, 43, 121
brotherhood, 21, 80, 85
Brown, John (Bedford), 88

Calvin, 87

Camara, Helder, 98, 104
Canterbury, Archbp. of, 18, 69, 90, 121
capitalism, bourgeois, 16
— state, 29
capitalist system, 29, 45, 88
caring, ch. 3 passim, 132
Carson, Rachel, 60–61
Celsus, 92
charity, 15, 41
Chavez, Cesar, 106
Chesterton, G. K., 29, 77–9, 109
Chile, 106
China, 28, 39, 48, 71, 110, 111
Christ and caring, ch. 3 passim
— and culture, 87–8
— and sharing, ch. 2 passim
— being in, 15, 85, 132
— fullness of, 16
— Lordship of, 131–2
— putting on, 88
— way of, 97, 100, 107, 125
  see also Jesus
Christian Aid, 42, 70, 73
— Marxists, 87
Christians and conservation, 56
— and violence, 100–107
— and way forward, ch. 10 passim
Church, 15, 25–7, 125–6
— and caring, 37, 41, 42, 125
— and class barriers, 91–2
— and education, 110–12
— and immigrants, 35–6
— and violence, 101–4
— and women, 94–5
— as Body of Christ, 50, 73
— government, 73
—, soldiers in, 102–3
Church, United Reformed, 104
Churches, British Council of, 5, 35, 42, 95, 122, 129
—, World Council of, 42, 73, 104, 107, 109

citizenship, 72
city-state, see polis
class barriers, 90–91, 125
co-decision industry, 74
Coketown, 58
commandments, great, 15, 108
—, Ten, 13
commitment, Christian, 36
common-wealth, 26
commonwealth, service of, 109
communal life, 13, 131
communication, 18, 77, 89
communications, 17, 114
community and education 109, 112
— and service, 48–9, 50, 52–3
—, koinonia, 23, 26–7
— of kibbutz, 27–8
— of Love, 14–15, 18, 32
— outreach, 37
—, sense of, 71–2, 122
Community Relations Commission, 35
competitive society, 110–1
comprehensive education, 72, 117
computers, 47–8
conscientisation, 112, 118
conservation, ch. 5 passim, 70, 122, 129
— in education, 118
Constantine, 101–2
co-operative society, 29, 110–11
Cornford, F. M., 116
corporate way of thinking, 15–16
convenant at Sinai, 13, 14
—, new, 14–15
craftsmanship, 47
Crates, 49
crime, 35–6, 89
Cromwell, Oliver, 85
crucifixion, 100, 104
Crusades, 102
cultural differences, 37, 88–9, 123, 125
Cyprus, 13

Dai Dong, 63

DDT, 58, 61
Dead Sea, 27
Deak, Ferenc, 105
decentralisation, ch. 6, passim
defence, spending on, 38
democracy, 70, 73, 76, 77, 78
D'Estaing, Giscard, 40
differentials of income, 22, 30, 53
dignity of work, 53–4, 73–4
disease, 18, 33, 53, 69
Distributism, 77
Dolci, Danilo, 11, 104, 106
Donne, John, 17
Douglass, James, 102
Dumont, René, 39, 67
dynamic element in reality, 81–3, 117

Ecologist, The, 62
economic programme, 18, 22, 62–3, 74, 96, 98, 123–4
Eden, 55
education, Christian, ch. 9, passim
—, English, 35, 72, 110, 124
—, Jewish, 46, 108
—, religious, 119
—, theology of, 108–9
—, university, 50–51, 72, 75, 111, 113–14
egalitarianism, 23, 90–95
Ehrlich, Paul, 64
Eisley, Loren, 55
Eliot, T. S., 87
élitism, 111
Ellul, Jacques, 99
Emerson, Ralph Waldo, 106–7
enemy, love of, 27
energy sources, 60, 67
Environment, Stockholm Conference on, 62–3
Erasmus, 103
Essenes, 14
Euripides, 118
exhaustion (of nature), 56, 58–60

exodus from Egypt, 11, 12–13, 82
expansion, ethos of, 62–4, 71–3
expertise, 28–9, 37

fear and love, 97, 107
fellowship, 23–4, 25, 85 (see also koinonia)
Fellowship of Reconciliation, 42, 76–7, 126, 131
Fergusson, Adam, 34
Finland, 93, 105
Fitchburg, Mass., 57
Fitzgerald, Brigid, 40
flexibility, 79, 81, 117
Flexner, Abraham, 50, 114
food policy, 39, 123
forgiveness, 37
— of sins, 11, 12
Fox, George, 11, 70, 89
France, 71, 72
Francis of Assisi, 11, 27, 56, 103, 105
Freire, Paolo, 112
Friends, Society of, 103
Fry, Elizabeth, 33

Gandhi, 47, 105
Ghana, 39
gifts, natural, 49–50
global action, 18, 38–43, 63–4, 69, 73
GNP, 38–9, 42
God's bounty, 12
— call, 11–12, 17, 44
— care and concern, 12, 65
— children, 42
— covenant, 13, 14–15, 73
— creation, 12, 55, 67, 82, 94
— grace, 22, 41
— image, 110
— Lordship of society, 67
— love, 71, 82, 84–5
— name and nature, 26, 28
— saving acts, 12–13
— way, 28, 89
— will, 18
— work, 44, 47, 54
— world, riches of, 22–3, 45

Goldsmith, Oliver, 85
grace, 22, 41
Greeks, ancient, 70, 72
Guatemala, 106
guerrillas, 14, 71
Guevara, Che, 99

Hebrew people, 13, 17
— slaves, 20
— thought, 15
Herbert, George, 48
history, dialectic of, 90
—, God, lord of, 12–13, 82, 108
—, lessons of, 71–2
—, philosophy of, 44, 47
—, theology of, 109
Hitler, Adolf, 99, 106
Hole, Dean, 56
hope, 11, 35, 112, 122
housing needs, 33–5, 90
humbleness, 11, 26, 28, 65, 85
Hungary, 105
hunger, 38, 39–40, 42, 69, 96, 123, 129
Hutchinson, Sir Joseph, 126, 130–31

ICI, 67
idleness, 46–7
Illich, Ivan, 112, 113
immigrant population, 33, 35–7
Incarnation, 50, 71
India, 32, 39
individual and ecology, 63
— and Lordship, 18
— as part of community, 15–16, 47
—, importance of, 11–12, 69–72, 121, 126
—, theology of, 109
individualism, excessive, 16–17
informed people, well-, 40–41
intellectualism, 46, 50–51
Internationalist, The New, 40
involvement, 23, 37, 42, 50, 125–6

Israel, 12, 13, 17, 26, 73, 131
—, new, 14–15, 131

Jenkins, David, 110
Jeremiah, 11, 14, 28
Jerusalem, 88, 100
Jesus, 11, 12, 21, 26, 37, 44, 46, 57, 108, 117, 128
—, way of, 14, 22–3, 83–4, 89, 100–101, 107
— and Son of Man, 16, 48
—, poverty of, 25
— and caring, 42, 65
— and suffering, 24, 44
— and riches, 22–3, 45
— and service, 48–9, 50
—, God in, 83
see also Christ
Jews see Hebrew people
job satisfaction, 35, 47, 49, 52
Jowett, 113
Jubilee, Year of, 20–21, 77
judgement, 13, 14, 15, 97
justice, social, 13, 15, 22, 28, 40, 41, 132

kibbutz, 27–8, 49
King, Martin Luther, 11, 104, 106
koinonia, 23, 25, 27, 132

Lapwood, Peter, 110
Lehrer, Tom, 57
leisure, 47
life, quality of, 13, ch. 5, passim
—, reverence for, 66
—, way of, 13, ch. 5, passim
life-style, 118–19, 123, 129–30
Ligt, Barthélemy de, 99
living standards, 38, 42, 52–3, 59, 64
Lordship of Christ, 131
— of God, 18
Los Angeles, 57
Loukes, Harold, 109

love *agape*, 14, 25, 26–7
— and Open Society, 90
— and violence, ch. 8, *passim*
— and work, 51
—, Jesus' way of, 83
—, Lordship of, 18
Loyola, Ignatius, 11
Luther, Martin, 11, 87
Luthuli, Albert, 106

Macaulay, 85
Macleod, George, 104
Malkin, Mart, 97
malnutrition, 64, 96
Manicheanism, 50
Marcellus, 102
Markham, Edwin, 84
Martha (and Mary), 47
Marx, Karl, 98, 114
mass-production, 47
Meadows, Dennis, 62
Melbourne, Lord, 85
Mellanby, Kenneth, 57
Mennonites, 103
Mersey, 57
Mesarovic, Mihajlo, 63
Mexico City, 112
Mill, J. S., 113
Milligan, Spike, 61
Milton Keynes, 72, 89
Minneapolis, 67
missionary endeavour, 32, 73
Moltmann, Jürgen, 107
morality of society, 80–81, 84
Morris, William, 41–2, 47
Mosaic law, 15
Moses, 11, 13, 14
Movement, 77
multi-national corporations, 78
Mumford, Lewis, 58
municipium, 71 (*see also polis*)
Musonius, Rufus, 53

Nansen, Fridtjof, 97
National Health Service, 52, 69
nationalism, 63, 72, 88

nations, judgement of, 15
neighbourliness, 36, 40
neighbour, love of, 27, 70–71
Neill, A. S., 117
Newman, Cardinal, 113
Newman, Oscar, 36
New Zealand, 93, 105
Nicholson, Max, 55
Niebuhr, H. Richard, 87
Niebuhr, Reinhold, 18
Niemöller, Martin, 104
Nigeria, 32, 99–100, 118, 126
Nobel, Alfred, 97
nonviolence, 14, ch. 8 *passim*
Nyerere, Julius, 45

Oduyoye, Amba, 126–8
Ojo, Gabriel, 54
Okara, Gabriel, 16
Oldham, J. H., 18
Oman, John, 26
Open Society, 79, ch. 7 *passim*, 116, 129, 131
— University, 47, 75–6
oppression, 97–100, 105
optimum size, 72
Origen, 101
Osborn, Fairfield, 58
Oxfam, 42, 70

parables, 12, 15, 21–2, 36–7, 45, 50, 55, 96
partnership, 23–4 (*see also koinonia*)
Paul (Saul), 11, 15, 16, 23–5, 45–6, 49, 53, 73, 83, 88, 100–101, 108, 131
peace, 14, 106–7 (*see also shalom*)
persons, 92, 109
Pestel, Eduard, 63
Peter (Simon), 11, 32, 37, 92, 100, 108
Plato, 81–2, 114, 117, 118
Platonism, 50, 80–81, 114
polis, 72 (*see also municipium*)
political institutions, 69–70, 77

— programme, 18, 42–3, 52
politics, great-power, 13–4
pollution 56–7, 62, 123–4
population, world, 18, 38–9, 58–60, 62–4
Porter, Sir George, 67
poverty, economic, 33, 35, 122
— of spirit, 33
power, temptation of, 83
— use of, 66–7, 69
powerlessness, 122, 123, 125
prayer, 37, 41, 54, 64, 83
privilege, 90–91, 98
productivity, 52
profit motive, 45, 67
prophetic role, 11, 17, 20–21, 28, 114, 122
Protestant ethic, 45

Quaker Peace Testimony, 73, 103, 105
Quislings, 14, 100

racism, 35–6, 70, 88, 97
Raven, Charles, 25
Reconciliation Quarterly, 5, 40, 67, 77
recycling, 67
Remnant, 17
Renaissance, 88, 114
repentance, 28, 128
reverence for life, 66
Revolution, Industrial, 88
revolutionary, 98, 100, 104, 107, 128
Rhine, 57
Richards, Ned, 105
riches, attitude to, 22–3, 45, 121
Ritschl, 87
Roberts, Michael, 60
Robinson, John, 85
Rollins, Rev. Metz, 81
Romans, ancient, 62, 71–2, 100
Rome, 24, 88, 105, 131
—, Church of, 91, 94
—, Club of, 62–3
Rondon, Candedo, 105
Rosebery, Lord, 70

Rossetti, D. G., 41–2
Rousseau, 114

sabbath, 20, 27, 129
Salvador, El, 106
Salvation Army, 33, 91
Sayers, Dorothy L., 54
Schumacher, E. G., 29–30
Schweitzer, Albert, 51, 65
Scott Bader Commonwealth, 29–30, 73–4, 75
Seale, Bobby, 106
service, 37–8, 48–9, 50
sex barrier, 92–5
Shackleton, Lord, 61
Shakespeare, 25, 45, 85, 111, 128
shalom, 42, 71, 127–8, 132
sharing, ch. 2 passim, 37–8, 131, 132
Shaw, Bernard, 46, 78
Shelter, 33–5
sin, propensity to, 46, 85, 89
Singh, Sundar, 105
size, 71–3, 74–5
skill, manual, 46
—, practical, 47, 108
slave trade, 32
'small is beautiful' 72–3, 74
socialism, 29, 78
society and education, 109–114
—, Christian, 86
—, deschooling, 112
—, kind of, 18–19, 22–3, 29, 67, 69–70, ch. 7 passim, 110, 126, 130, 132
—, permissive, 89
—, pluralist, 88, 125
Sorokin, Pitimir, 98
South Africa, 106
Spirit, work of, 18, 89, 108, 125, 131
—, God in, 83–4, 122

Squire, J. C., 102
Stevenson, R. L., 40
stewardship, 55, 130
Strong, Maurice, 62–3
structure of society, 18, 98, 109–10, 126
Studdert-Kennedy, G. A., 93–4
suffering, 14, 44, 100
Sweden, 52
Swomley, John M., 98–100, 106

Tanzania, 111
Tao, 83
Tawney, R. H., 45
taxation, 62, 67
teamwork, 47, 52, 75–6
technology, 47–8, 64–6, 88
Telegraph, The Daily, 90–91
Telemachus, 105
Temple, William, 83–4
temptations of Jesus, 83–4, 100, 102
Tennyson, 119–20
Terence, 40
Teresa, Mother, 11, 33
Tertullian, 87, 101
tithes, 39
togetherness, 24 (see also koinonia)
Tokyo, 57
toleration, 88
Tolstoy, 87, 117–18
Torah, 13, 14, 84
Torres, Camilo, 99
Toynbee, Arnold, 44
Trenton, 72
Trevelyan, G. M., 92
truth, 118
Turgeniev, 85–6

Ubico, Jorge, 106
UN, 73, 93
UNA, 40, 42
UN agencies, 18, 38, 43, 69

unemployment, 33, 35, 51, 52–3, 90–91, 122, 125
UNESCO, 115–16
unpleasant jobs, 53
USA, official policy of, 38–9, 43, 81
—, society in, 39, 45, 57, 61, 72, 80–81, 97, 106
USSR, 80–81, 93

Vergil, 44
Vietnam War, 97, 118
violence, 14, ch. 8 passim, 122, 132
— of system, 98
Vogt, William, 59
Volvo, 52

war, 60, 80, 97
—, just, 102–3, 104
War on Want, 42
wealth, pursuit of, 22, 29, 45, 121
Weber, Max, 45
Welfare State, 33
Wells, H. G., 78
Wesley, John, 62
wholeness, see shalom
Williams, Eric, 33
Willkie, Wendell, 69
Wilson, Des, 33–4
Wilson, Harold, 40
Wilson, Rev. H. O., 66
wisdom, 70, 91, 108, 119
women, role of, 49, 92–5
Wood, Alex, 30
work, ch. 4 passim, 73–4, 131
World Health Organisation, 69
World, Third, 39–41, 52, 123
— view, 18, 38–43, 63–4, 69, 73, 123, 130

Zealots, 14, 100